Rogues in Royal Robes

Exploring the lives of some Old Testament kings and the times in which they lived

Dr A. J. Monty White

DayOne

© Day One Publications 2020

ISBN 978-1-84625-677-6
Scriptures and additional materials quoted are from
the Good News Bible © 1994 published by the Bible Societies/
HarperCollins Publishers Ltd UK, Good News Bible© American Bible
Society 1966, 1971, 1976, 1992. Used with permission;
Holy Bible, New International Version® Anglicized, NIV® Copyright ©
1979, 1984, 2011;
the anglicized edition of the ESV Bible copyright © 2002 Collins, part
of HarperCollins Publishers;
the New King James Version (NKJV)®. Copyright © 1982 by Thomas
Nelson, Inc. Used by permission. All rights reserved; and
the Authorized (King James) Version (AV), Crown copyright.

British Library Cataloguing in Publication Data available

Published by Day One Publications
Ryelands Road, Leominster, HR6 8NZ
Telephone 01568 613 740 FAX 01568 611 473
email—sales@dayone.co.uk
web site—www.dayone.co.uk

Cover design by Kathryn Chedgzoy
Printed by 4edge

For Dr Michael Bennett,
who first introduced me to these rogues in royal
robes, and who first explained the gospel to me.

ENDORSEMENTS

It is a privilege and pleasure to commend Dr Monty White's Rogues in Royal Robes *to the wider Christian public. Having been engrossed by the manuscript in its pre-publication stage, I can vouch for the fact that you are about to embark on the most enlightening and interesting elucidation of an often neglected era of Old Testament history—the life and times, and ups and downs, of the kings of Israel and Judah. Gaps in your biblical knowledge are shortly to be filled, and more than one or two puzzles and perplexities resolved!*

Timothy Cross Th.D., Litt.D., Christian author and preacher

British Prime Minister David Lloyd George once admitted that although he could hardly name half a dozen kings of England and Wales, he knew all the kings of Israel. Though many Christians today would have to confess the same ignorance of this country's kings, how many can say they know all the kings of Israel, still less who they were, what they did or their significance? In this book, Dr Monty White helpfully dispels our ignorance and presents a treasure trove of valuable information about the ancient Hebrew kings. Rogues in Royal Robes *ought to be on the shelves of all Christian ministers and everyone who is serious about understanding the Bible.*

Mike Moore, Former General Secretary, Christian Witness to Israel

It is a great privilege to commend this book on some of the Old Testament kings. Monty White's lament that there is widespread ignorance of Old Testament history amongst many Christians is, alas, too true. This book helps to address this problem and to fill in the details for those whose knowledge of Old Testament history is either sketchy or non-existent. In putting into the reader's hands the results of archaeological discoveries (some of which can be seen in the British Museum in London) and the fruit of the research carried out by various scholars in this field (as well as that of his own research), the author demonstrates the historical accuracy and trustworthiness of the Old Testament. Every reader will surely be the better informed about the fascinating period covered by this vade mecum. Not only does each chapter end with a helpful summary but there are also spiritual applications for us today. The best is left until last, where we read of the perfect king, Jesus Christ. What better way to end! I heartily commend it.

Rev. Stephen Clark, recently retired pastor of Free School Court Evangelical Church, Bridgend, and lecturer in Systematic Theology at the London Seminary

Contents

D r A. J. Monty White was converted to Christianity from atheism in 1964 when he was an undergraduate student at what was then the University College of Wales, Aberystwyth—now Aberystwyth University. One of the reasons why Monty started to take the Bible seriously was because he became convinced that the historical events recorded in the Old Testament actually took place, many being corroborated by Assyrian and Babylonian records discovered by archaeologists. This knowledge turned him from an atheist into someone who believed that there was a God and that the Bible could be trusted. One night in February 1964 Monty heard the gospel message and as a result turned to the Lord Jesus Christ for salvation through his death on Calvary's cross. His life has never been the same since!

Monty is a graduate of the University of Wales, having obtained his BSc in 1967 and been awarded a PhD in 1970 for his research in the field of gas kinetics. After a further two years of chemical research at Aberystwyth, Monty moved to Cardiff, where he held a number of senior administrative posts at Cardiff University until September 2000, when he became the Chief Executive of Answers in Genesis (UK/Europe), a post which he held until July 2008. Monty then returned to South Wales and with his wife, Irene, set up Biblical Foundations. He had an itinerant ministry speaking and preaching until Irene became ill with cancer, when Monty had to curtail his ministry in order to care for her. Irene finally went to be with the Lord in March 2018.

Monty has written a number of books, booklets and pamphlets dealing with the subject of creation and evolution. He has also contributed chapters on creation to other books and has had dozens of articles published in magazines and journals worldwide. His writings have been translated into Dutch, French, German, Portuguese, Russian and Swedish. Monty has spoken and lectured extensively not only in the UK but also in many European countries, as well as in Hong Kong and the USA. From 1983 until 2001, Monty was a guest lecturer on the subject of the Bible and Science at the State Independent Theological University of Basel, Switzerland.

Since leaving Answers in Genesis (UK/Europe), Monty has developed a number of talks about the history that is found in the Bible and how much of this history has been corroborated by archaeological discoveries that have been made in the Middle East. This book is, however, Monty's first venture into the written word about biblical history and the corroborative archaeological findings that show how, in matters pertaining to history, the Bible can be trusted.

It is a privilege and pleasure to commend Dr Monty White's *Rogues in Royal Robes* to the wider Christian public. Having been engrossed by the manuscript in its pre-publication stage, I can vouch for the fact that you are about to embark on the most enlightening and interesting elucidation of an often neglected era of Old Testament history—the life and times, and ups and downs, of the kings of Israel and Judah. Gaps in your biblical knowledge are shortly to be filled, and more than one or two puzzles and perplexities resolved!

Monty states that one of his purposes in writing was to 'rouse your interest in the Old Testament'. He certainly achieved this purpose with me. The charts and tables are most helpful, and the contemporary applications most relevant. Also, his sharing of extra-biblical insights into the era—gained from his extensive archaeological research—will most surely confirm your faith in the absolute truth and historical veracity of the divinely inspired volume.

The Old Testament is the necessary backcloth to an understanding of its fulfilment in the Christ of the New Testament. It is thus fitting that Monty concludes this compact book by focusing our attention on the focus of all Scripture, the Lord Jesus Christ, comparing and contrasting the King of kings with the imperfect kings which preceded him. When you reach the end of the book, therefore, it will be time to stop reading and to start worshipping.

Timothy Cross Th.D., Litt.D.
Christian author and preacher

For a good number of years I have toyed with the idea of writing a book about some of the kings of the Northern Kingdom of Israel and the Southern Kingdom of Judah that we read about in the Old Testament. However, the idea really took hold when I gave a couple of sermons about the life and times of King Joash at a small church in the South Wales Valleys about a decade ago. As I preached about the life of this particular king, I realized that members of the congregation were not familiar with any of the historical background to King Joash's reign—in fact, they were not even aware of *when* Joash reigned! I also realized that they were only able to follow the story of his reign because I had prepared, using PowerPoint, a detailed family tree (with dates!) so they were able to determine easily the family relationships of each of the characters in the story. Without such a family tree, they would have been totally lost.

Since beginning to write this book, I have become increasingly conscious that many Christians are generally uninformed about the history of the nation of Israel from the time of the exodus, when Moses led them out of captivity in Egypt, to the Babylonian exile, when they were taken into captivity in Babylon. I have also realized that, in general, Christians do not have any idea of the events that were occurring at the time in the other Middle Eastern countries that constituted Israel's neighbours, allies and enemies. This was brought home to me at a Christian conference at which I spoke, where not one person in the audience was able to tell me when King David lived, when the city of Samaria was destroyed and by which enemy, or when Jerusalem was sacked and by which army!

This is a reflection of the decline in the study of biblical history in our Sunday schools, and of biblical history and archaeology in our schools, universities, theological seminaries and Bible colleges. These studies are often considered unnecessary to the understanding of biblical Israel and her faith and so, too, of the Christian faith. As a result, these courses have been replaced by more 'stylish' courses in liberation theology; feminism and the Bible; and literary criticism, including structuralism, semiotics, rhetorical criticism, and even more esoteric studies.[1] The outcome is that pastors are not grounded in Old Testament history and so are unable to teach it to their congregations.

I believe that many Christians think that the Old Testament is no longer relevant to them and so simply do not read it and therefore teach it. I hope that this book will rouse your interest in the Old Testament and cause you to study it for yourself. To test your knowledge of Old Testament history, allow me to ask two simple questions: Do you know the historical background that explains the political reason why King Ahab of the Northern Kingdom of Israel was married to Jezebel? Are you aware of the religious background giving significance to Elijah's challenging the prophets of Baal to a contest of bringing fire down from heaven? If you cannot answer these two questions, you are in good company. I trust, however, that by the time you have read this book, you will be able not only to give answers to these two questions, but also to notice comparisons between the lives of the kings of the Northern Kingdom of Israel and the Southern Kingdom of Judah and life today in the twenty-first century.

Maybe you don't like history, and dates confuse you. Don't worry, again you are in good company! I hated history in school and could not wait to give it up so that I could devote more of my time to the study of the sciences, which I loved. Yet when I became interested in the Bible, I realized that I had to try to understand much of the history that I read in the Old Testament. This was so that I could appreciate what was going on in the land of Israel (as well as in the lands of her neighbours) and which kings were reigning at the time when the prophets uttered their prophecies and their messages from God.

There are, therefore, a number of reasons why I have written this book. It is so readers can appreciate:

- the overall history of Israel from the time of its first king, Saul, to the Babylonian exile;
- that the kings who are mentioned in the books of Kings and Chronicles in the Old Testament were real historical individuals and not the mythical monarchs they once were thought to be;
- the overall chronology of the events that we read about in the books of Kings and Chronicles in the Old Testament and why we can be certain about when the kings mentioned in these books actually lived;
- that the histories of the Northern Kingdom of Israel and the Southern Kingdom of Judah that are recorded in the Bible are not in any doubt and that anyone who says otherwise is speaking from a position of ignorance, not being aware of the enormous contribution that has been made in the last century by archaeological discoveries in the Middle East;
- that the events and time periods recorded in the books of Kings and Chronicles in the Old Testament are not at variance with each other and are not at variance with the events and chronologies recorded in the countries surrounding the Northern Kingdom of Israel and the Southern Kingdom of Judah, chronologies which have been fixed by the dates on which eclipses took place—the dates of these eclipses having been confirmed by astronomical calculations;
- the consequences of the events that occurred in the lives of four of the kings who are mentioned in these historical books—Omri, Ahab, Jehu and Joash—whose lives are studied in detail in this book;
- and, finally, the origins of the Samaritans and, consequently, why the Jews tended to view them with contempt at the time of Christ.

It is customary in a book such as this to mention the people who have been an inspiration or encouragement to the author. There are two people above all others who warrant such a mention. One is Dr Michael Bennett, for it was he who initiated my interest in Old Testament history when we were both undergraduates in the 1960s at what was then the University College of Wales, Aberystwyth (now Aberystwyth University). When I first met Michael, I was an atheist who thought that the Bible was a book of myths, legends and fairy stories. He patiently took me through many chapters of the books of Kings and Chronicles and explained to me that the history contained in them could be trusted and that many of the stories we read in these books have been corroborated by Assyrian and Babylonian records discovered by archaeologists. I am indebted to Michael not only for this, but also for making me realize that the whole of the Bible can be trusted. I am also grateful to him for explaining the way of salvation to me and praying with me as I repented of my sins and trusted the Lord Jesus Christ as my Saviour in February 1964. I have the pleasure of dedicating this book to him.

The other person I want to thank is my dear departed wife, Irene. She encouraged me to write this book and made me promise her that after her death I would continue to write it, as it was her wish that others would know the kings of Israel, Judah and Assyria that are written about in the Old Testament as well as we do in our family.

Dr A. J. Monty White

South Wales

NOTES

1 William G. Dever, *What Did the Biblical Writers Know and When Did They Know It?* (Grand Rapids, MI / Cambridge: Eerdmans, 2002), p. 3.

A brief history of the kingdoms of Israel and Judah

We are probably all familiar with the story of the exodus—how, under Moses' leadership, God led the children of Israel out of the land of Egypt after sending a series of plagues on Egypt, the last one being the killing of the firstborn. God told Moses that the children of Israel could escape this tenth and last plague by sacrificing a male lamb and sprinkling its blood on the doorposts and lintels of their houses. The Lord would then pass over their homes without killing any of their firstborn. This was the first Passover, and in 1 Corinthians 5:7 the Apostle Paul tells us that the Lord Jesus Christ is our Passover Lamb sacrificed for us. Just as the Passover lambs were slain, so the Lord Jesus Christ has been slain. And just as the blood of the Passover lambs had to be applied to the doorposts and lintels of the houses of the Israelites in order for them to be saved from the judgement of the Lord, so the blood of the Lord Jesus Christ has to be applied to our lives in order for us to be saved.

Moses led the children of Israel through the Red Sea and then, because of their unbelief and lack of trust in the Lord, they spent forty years wandering in the wilderness, until there was a new generation of Israelites who trusted God. During these wilderness years, God did not forsake Israel—he miraculously provided them with water to drink and manna and quails to eat. Under the leadership of Joshua, the Israelites entered 'the Promised Land'—the territory from the east bank of the Jordan Valley right up to the Mediterranean coast: the area we know today as Israel and Palestine.

It took about fifty years for the Israelites to gradually defeat the

Canaanites who occupied the land at the time. The story of how the children of Israel conquered and settled into the land of Canaan is complex and is covered in the books of Joshua and Judges. This phase of Israel's history has been ably summed up by Brian Edwards: 'This was a messy and miserable period during which the unhappy cycle of events was that tribes squabbled among themselves, broke the laws of God and suffered the penalty. Periods of oppression by their enemies were interspersed with periods of peace led by one of the eighteen judges including the well-known figures of Deborah, Gideon and Samson.'[1]

The book of Judges ends with the sentence: 'There was no king in Israel at that time. Everyone did whatever they pleased' (Judg. 21:25, GNT).

Saul, the first king of Israel

I have given this book the title *Rogues in Royal Robes* and Saul, the first king of Israel, was one such rogue who ended up wearing royal robes. The first book of Samuel opens with the story of the birth, and subsequent calling, of Samuel to be a prophet (God's mouthpiece) to the nation of Israel. Towards the end of Samuel's ministry, the Israelites asked Samuel if, instead of having God to rule over them, they could have a king, as other nations had. In other words, they wanted to change from being a theocracy to a monarchy. In 1 Samuel 12:19 it is recorded that the people realized they had sinned by asking God for a king, and yet, in spite of this, God did not refuse their plea but, through Samuel, warned them of the consequences of their having a king to rule over them (see 1 Sam. 8:11–18). He warned them that their king would take their sons for his army, their daughters for his household, their fields, vineyards and olive groves, a tenth of their farm produce and sheep, and the finest of their servants. In other words, their kings would indeed be rogues, as we shall see that they were.

In spite of this, the Israelites still demanded a king, and under God's guidance Samuel anointed Saul as the first king of Israel. Saul was the people's choice—he was handsome and stood head and shoulders above everyone else. However, the good-looking, tallest person is not always the best candidate for the job, as Samuel and the rest of the Israelites were to find out to their cost.

We are able to determine the dates of the reign of King Saul from the information given in Acts 13:21, where we read that he reigned for forty years. His successor, the great King David, began his reign in 1010 BC, so King Saul reigned from 1050 to 1010 BC.

Even at the beginning of his reign King Saul behaved badly and sinned against the Lord. Samuel had told Saul to go to Gilgal and to wait for him for seven days, when Samuel would join him and offer sacrifices. Saul went to Gilgal but, in the meantime, the Philistines gathered a large force at Michmash and launched such a strong attack on the Israelites that some of them hid in caves, among the rocks and in pits and wells, while others even crossed the River Jordan into the territories of Gad and Gilead. In the meantime, Saul was still at Gilgal, and he waited seven days there for Samuel to arrive, as instructed by Samuel. The people, however, started to desert Saul, so he offered a burnt offering as a sacrifice to the Lord. Now, Saul was a member of the tribe of Benjamin and, by offering a burnt sacrifice to the Lord, completely disregarded God's Law, for this was something only someone from the priestly tribe of Levi was allowed to do. Samuel arrived just as Saul was finishing offering the burnt offering, and he was furious. Samuel told Saul in no uncertain terms that the Lord was angry and that, as a result, Saul's kingdom would not continue and the Lord would seek a man after his own heart to rule his people.

Saul did not learn his lesson; he did not repent, for he later disobeyed God big time. In 1 Samuel 15 we read the story of the prophet Samuel telling King Saul that God was going to use him and his army to punish the Amalekites for what their ancestors had done by opposing the

Israelites when they came out of Egypt. King Saul was told: 'Now go, attack the Amalekites and totally destroy all that belongs to them. Do not spare them; put to death men and women, children and infants, cattle and sheep, camels and donkeys' (1 Sam. 15:1, NIV).

It must be understood that this was not ethnic cleansing but ethical or moral cleansing. Saul and his army defeated the Amalekites but, although Saul's instructions were clear, he did not obey the Lord's command. He did not kill the king (Agag) and he allowed his soldiers to keep the best sheep and cattle and anything else that was good, while destroying only what was useless and worthless. Saul then lied to Samuel, saying that he had obeyed the Lord's command! This resulted in Samuel telling Saul that the Lord had rejected Saul as king of Israel.

At the end of King Saul's reign, the Philistines made war with Israel again and assembled at Shunem while King Saul led his army to Mount Gilboa. When Saul saw the Philistine army, he was terrified and he asked the Lord what to do. We are told that the Lord did not answer him by the usual methods he used in those days—by dreams, the use of Urim and Thummim[2] or prophets. Now, after the prophet Samuel had died, King Saul did do one thing that was commendable: he had forced all the mediums and spiritists to leave Israel. But because Saul was not getting an answer to his prayer he committed an unforgivable sin: he consulted a witch—something which was punishable by death under the Law (Lev. 20:27). He asked his officials to find a medium—a witch—who still lived in Israel whom he could consult and who could answer his prayer. One such person was the witch of Endor. When Saul disguised himself and visited this witch, Samuel appeared to Saul to tell him again that the Lord had taken the kingdom away from him. Furthermore, Samuel told him that on the following day, Saul and his sons would be killed in battle. And that is what happened: Saul was wounded in a battle with the Philistines that took place the day after he had consulted the witch. Saul then committed suicide by throwing himself on his own sword. And so ended the life of the first king of Israel.

David and Solomon

David had already been anointed king by the prophet Samuel and, after Saul died, David ruled in Hebron over Judah for seven and a half years and then in Jerusalem over all Israel and Judah for thirty-three years. David was a man of war and eventually brought peace to Israel by defeating the Philistines and subduing the other enemies of Israel who lived in the Promised Land. David was thirty years old when he began to reign and he reigned for forty years, from 1010 to 970 BC; when he died, his son Solomon became king.

I have often asked church leaders if they would have someone like King David as a leader or even a music group leader in their churches—after all, he was a king and he wrote many of the Psalms, some of the most beautiful and uplifting songs of praise and worship that have ever been written. These leaders have inevitably answered in the affirmative. I have then reminded them of David's dreadful sin—how he committed adultery with Bathsheba and then, when he got her pregnant, conspired to get her husband, Uriah the Hittite, killed in battle so he could marry her. Church leaders have usually hesitated at this point and then said that they cannot see how they could possibly have such a person in any leadership role in their churches. Yet this man, David, is held up in the Bible over and over again as a king that other kings should emulate and try to follow. Why is this? Because David truly repented of his sin and followed the Lord faithfully all the days of his life. Surely there is a lesson for Christians here. Should we not learn to forgive those who sin *if* they have truly repented of their sin? In fact, in the historical books of the Old Testament, we read over and over again that king so-and-so did evil, not as David did, or that king so-and-so did good, as David did.

King David is held up as an example of a king who served God with all his mind, heart, soul and will.

Until the 1990s King David was known only from the Bible. Then in 1993 excavations at Tel Dan in the north of Israel uncovered a stone erected by a king of Damascus to commemorate his victory over two enemy kings. This stone has the inscription *BYTDWD* on it, which has been translated 'house of David'. This inscription dates from the ninth century BC as it had been sealed off by a later Assyrian destruction layer that has been firmly dated to 733/32 BC. This is incontrovertible proof that King David is not some mythological monarch but was a real king who existed in history and whose kingdom was known about by those who lived shortly after him.

The child born to Bathsheba as a result of King David's adultery died. King David then married Bathsheba, and the child of that union was the great King Solomon. King David wanted to build a temple in Jerusalem so that the Ark of the Covenant could be housed in it—so that God would have a dwelling place and the Ark would not be kept in a tent. But God indicated to King David that he was not to build the temple because he was a man of war; this task was to be undertaken by his son, Solomon. King Solomon duly undertook this task towards the beginning of his reign, and he reigned over Israel for a period of forty years, from 970 to 930 BC.

Towards the end of his reign King Solomon had seven hundred wives and three hundred concubines as a result of his loving foreign women. These women, however, turned his heart away from the Lord and he began to worship idols. Because of King Solomon's idolatry, the Lord sent the prophet Ahijah to Jeroboam, one of King Solomon's trusted officials who was also one of his building foremen, to tell him that he would reign over Israel's ten northern tribes. When King Solomon heard about this, he tried to kill Jeroboam, but Jeroboam escaped to Egypt and stayed there until King Solomon died.

Civil war in Israel

When King Solomon died, his son, Rehoboam, became king. Jeroboam returned from Egypt and the people of the northern tribes sent for him; they all then went together to King Rehoboam and told him that his father King Solomon had treated them harshly, imposing upon them high taxes and forced labour for building projects. They asked him if he was prepared to lighten their burden; if so, they would serve him in return. He asked for three days in which to consider their request. King Rehoboam first consulted the older men who had advised his father King Solomon; they advised him to give a favourable response, saying that if he did so the people would serve him loyally. King Rehoboam ignored their advice and instead turned to the young men who had grown up with him and who were now his advisers. When he asked them how he should answer the people, they answered with these oft-quoted words from 1 Kings 12:10–11: 'My little finger is thicker than my father's waist. My father laid on you a heavy yoke; I will make it even heavier. My father scourged you with whips; I will scourge you with scorpions' (NIV).

This is how King Rehoboam answered the people when they returned to him after three days. As a result, the northern tribes rallied around Jeroboam, crowned him as their king and started a new kingdom—the Northern Kingdom of Israel. The two tribes in the south of Israel, Judah and Benjamin, remained loyal to King Rehoboam and formed the Southern Kingdom of Judah.

We often think of there having been twelve tribes of Israel and after the civil war there being a ten–two split, as I have outlined above. However, it was a little more complicated than that. Jacob, who had later been renamed Israel, had twelve sons, and each son gave rise to a tribe, each of which was given an area in the Promised Land. However, Joseph's two sons, Ephraim and Manasseh, were each given their own tribal area; and to complicate matters even further, Levi was *not* given any tribal area—

members of the tribe of Levi were scattered throughout the land because they were priests with what could be described as civic as well as religious duties.

A careful study of the civil war that occurred in Israel at the time of King Rehoboam actually resulted in the following tribes living in the following kingdoms:

THE NORTHERN KINGDOM OF ISRAEL	THE SOUTHERN KINGDOM OF JUDAH
Asher	Judah
Dan	Benjamin
Ephraim	Simeon
Gad	Levi—because all the Levites abandoned their homes and property in the Northern Kingdom of Israel and moved south to the Southern Kingdom of Judah because King Jeroboam rejected them as priests of the Lord as soon as he set up his own religion (2 Chr. 11:13–14).
Issachar	Those from every other tribe of Israel who set their hearts on seeking the Lord, the God of Israel, the God of their fathers (2 Chr. 11:16).
Manasseh	
Naphtali	
Reuben	
Zebulun	

So in fact it was a nine–four split, with some taken off the nine and some added onto the four!

The Northern Kingdom of Israel

As we have seen, Jeroboam was the first king of the Northern Kingdom of Israel. He realized very quickly that he had a serious religious problem on his hands, for the centre of worship for all the children of Israel was the temple in Jerusalem, which was located in the Southern Kingdom of Judah. King Jeroboam was afraid that if the Israelites in the Northern Kingdom of Israel crossed the border into the Southern Kingdom of Judah to visit the temple, they would transfer their allegiance to King Rehoboam, who was king of the Southern Kingdom of Judah. King Jeroboam's solution to this problem was to construct two golden calves and to place them in the Northern Kingdom of Israel, in the cities of Dan in the north and Bethel in the south, and to inform the people that these were their gods who had brought them out of Egypt. What an example of fake news! King Jeroboam also built places of worship on hilltops and chose priests from families who were *not* of the tribe of Levi. This was why the Levites abandoned their homes and property in the Northern Kingdom of Israel and moved south to the Southern Kingdom of Judah. What was King Jeroboam's loss was King Rehoboam's gain and strengthened the Southern Kingdom of Judah.

The monarchical line in the Northern Kingdom of Israel was not from father to son, but was often overturned by assassinations, murders, court plots and even a suicide! During the period from 930 BC, when King Jeroboam began to reign, and 723 BC, when the Assyrians finally destroyed Samaria, the capital city of the Northern Kingdom of Israel, there were nineteen kings and the line was broken eight times. In seven of these, the king was murdered by his successor, while the eighth committed suicide. A summary of these events is shown in Table 1 on page 27, and we will be looking at the lives of three of these kings—Omri, Ahab and Jehu—in detail in chapters 3, 4 and 5, respectively.

After King Solomon's death in 930 BC the kingdom of Assyria became increasingly powerful and, within a hundred years, King Jehu of the

Northern Kingdom of Israel was paying tribute to King Shalmaneser III of Assyria in 841 BC. A hundred years later, King Tiglath-Pileser III of Assyria invaded the Northern Kingdom of Israel and as a consequence some of the northern tribes were taken captive to the northern border area of the Assyrian Empire. Then for nearly three years King Shalmaneser V, King Tiglath-Pileser III's son and successor, besieged Samaria, the capital city of the Northern Kingdom of Israel. It fell in 723 BC, and his successor, his brother Sargon II, took more of the people captive and moved them to the River Gozan area and to the cities of the Medes. From 721 BC, King Sargon II and his successors (especially his grandson, King Esarhaddon, and his great-grandson, King Ashurbanipal) continued the established Assyrian policy of repopulation. At this time more people from the Northern Kingdom of Israel were moved to the River Gozan area and the cities of the Medes, and the depopulated land of northern Israel was repopulated with foreign peoples who later became the Samaritans of the Lord Jesus Christ's time. Thus the Northern Kingdom of Israel ceased to exist and its peoples were taken away from the Promised Land and into captivity as a result of their disobedience and idolatry, just as the Lord had warned them would happen in Deuteronomy chapter 28.

The Southern Kingdom of Judah

We have seen that after the civil war King Rehoboam ended up with the tribes of Judah, Benjamin, Simeon, Levi and a few people from some of the tribes from the Northern Kingdom of Israel. He established his kingdom but, after three years, he abandoned the Law of the Lord, and subsequently his kingdom was invaded by King Shishak of Egypt. The Bible records in 2 Chronicles 12:3–4 that Shishak's army was composed of twelve hundred chariots, sixty thousand horsemen and more soldiers than could be counted, including Libyan, Sukkite and Sudanese troops, and that they captured the fortified cities of the Southern Kingdom of

TABLE 1: THE KINGS OF THE NORTHERN KINGDOM OF ISRAEL	
Nine dynasties—nineteen kings	
Eight of these kings (42% of them) met their death by violence.	Seven of these kings were assassinated by their successors and one committed suicide.
1st Dynasty: Jeroboam I; Nadab	Nabad was assassinated by Baasha (1 Kings 15:27)
2nd Dynasty: Baasha; Elah	Elah was assassinated by Zimri while Elah was getting drunk (1 Kings 16:10)
3rd Dynasty: Zimri	Zimri reigned only a week[3] before committing suicide at Tirzah (1 Kings 16:18)
4th Dynasty: Omri; Ahab; Ahaziah; Jehoram	Jehoram was killed by Jehu (2 Kings 9:24)
5th Dynasty: Jehu; Jehoahaz; Joash; Jeroboam II; Zechariah	Zechariah was assassinated by Shallum (2 Kings 15:10)
6th Dynasty: Shallum	Shallum was assassinated by Menahem (2 Kings 15:14)
7th Dynasty: Menahem; Pekahiah	Pekahiah was assassinated by Pekah (2 Kings 15:25)
8th Dynasty: Pekah	Pekah was assassinated by Hoshea (2 Kings 15:30)
9th Dynasty: Hoshea	
The lives of these Old Testament kings of the Northern Kingdom of Israel make depressing reading; the majority led the children of Israel (God's chosen people) away from the Lord.	

Judah and advanced as far as Jerusalem. Later, via the prophet Shemaiah, the Lord told King Rehoboam and the leaders of the Southern Kingdom of Judah that, as they had abandoned the Lord, so he now had abandoned them to King Shishak.

In general, the kings and the people in the Southern Kingdom of Judah did not learn from their own mistakes nor from the mistakes made by their neighbours in the Northern Kingdom of Israel—not even when they saw their northern brothers and sisters being taken into captivity by the Assyrians. Not even this made them repent and turn to the Lord and serve him with all their hearts and minds. There were a few kings of the Southern Kingdom of Judah who faithfully served the Lord, but these were the exception rather than the rule. Two of these worth mentioning are King Hezekiah and his grandson, Josiah. However, in general, the kings continued to sin against the Lord and to lead the people away from serving him. Yet amazingly, the monarchical line in the Southern Kingdom of Judah was from father to son, and so the line of the throne of David survived.

The history of the last twenty years of the Southern Kingdom of Judah makes sad reading. From 605 to 586 BC the Babylonians led by King Nebuchadnezzar invaded the Southern Kingdom of Judah several times. Each time, not only was the land invaded, but the city of Jerusalem was also attacked and damaged by the Babylonian army, and with each invasion the Babylonians took more of the people from the Southern Kingdom of Judah captive back to Babylon. The city of Jerusalem was finally sacked on 10 July 586 BC, one hundred years after the death of Hezekiah. The people from the Southern Kingdom of Judah who were taken into captivity in Babylon began to return to their homeland some seventy years later under the Persian kings. The events surrounding the return of the people from this exile (as it became known) and the rebuilding of Jerusalem are recorded in the books of Ezra and Nehemiah. The descendants of the people who returned from Babylon were the Jews of the New Testament.

Summary and conclusion

The history of the children of Israel—from their journey out of captivity in Egypt to the Promised Land, to their life under the judges, their first king, Saul, and then his successor, King David, and his son, Solomon, and the subsequent civil war which occurred when King Solomon died—is not very easy to follow. However, the subsequent histories of the resulting Northern Kingdom of Israel and Southern Kingdom of Judah are extremely difficult to determine. The kingdom of Assyria grew in strength and eventually carried the people of the Northern Kingdom of Israel into captivity, repopulating the land with foreigners who became the Samaritans of the Lord Jesus Christ's time. Eventually, the Babylonians invaded the Southern Kingdom of Judah and carried them into captivity in Babylon. They began to return some seventy years later. All this is difficult to take in, but one thing is very clear: the destruction of Israel and her subsequent captivity was the consequence of her sin and idolatry.

NOTES

1 Brian H. Edwards, *Saul and Sons: Decline and Fallout in the Family of Israel's First King* (Leominster: Day One, 2010), pp. 5–6.

2 Urim and Thummim are two untranslated Hebrew words which might mean 'lights and perfections'. They refer to some kind of stones or tokens which the high priest of Israel used for discovering the will of God. Theories abound, but most guess that they were something like dice or coins which had to land upright or upside down as an answer to prayer.

3 The phrase 'A week is a long time in politics' is attributed to the British Prime Minister Harold Wilson.

Making sense of the history of the kingdoms of Israel and Judah

It is my hope that you will find this book a help in understanding the storylines and the sequences of events that we come across when we read the history of the United Kingdom of Israel, the Northern Kingdom of Israel and the Southern Kingdom of Judah in the Old Testament. In order to appreciate how we can bring clarity to the narratives we encounter in the historical books of the Old Testament, we first of all have to recognize that there are a number of difficulties we run into when we try to make sense of the history of God's people as recounted in these books. The first problem we encounter is that no dates are given in the narratives, so we often find it difficult to follow the story, especially if we are reading the life story of a king in the book of Kings as well as in the book of Chronicles. Another complication is that we are often unfamiliar with ancient Middle Eastern geography and place names, and frequently the names of countries, areas, towns and villages that are used in the Old Testament are totally different from the names that are used today in the twenty-first century.

The third area of difficulty which leads to confusion is the names that are used to talk about God's people in the Old Testament. Sometimes the Israelites are called 'Hebrews' and sometimes 'the house of Jacob'. There are times when 'Israel' is used to refer to the whole of Israel, and other times when just the Northern Kingdom of Israel is meant. Sometimes the Northern Kingdom of Israel is called 'Samaria'—and this should not be confused with the city of Samaria! Although 'Judah' usually refers to the

Southern Kingdom of Judah, sometimes it refers just to that area of the Southern Kingdom of Judah occupied by the tribe of Judah. No wonder many of us find reading and understanding the historical parts of the Old Testament difficult and confusing!

The fourth problem we encounter is our lack of familiarity with the names of the kings mentioned in the Bible—especially when they have more than one name and the writer recounts episodes in their lives using two (or sometimes even three) of their names on different occasions, without actually spelling out to the reader that it is the same person! This results in the reader sometimes not realizing that the stories are about the same king and thinking that the writer is describing the exploits of two (or even three) different kings who lived at the same time. Finally, there is the problem of unfamiliarity with the names of the kings of the countries that were the neighbours and enemies of God's people at the time. This is particularly true when we encounter the names of some of the Assyrian kings.

In this chapter we will look at each of these problems in turn and see if we can find solutions that will enable us to start to understand more fully the history that is recorded for us in the books of Kings and Chronicles in the Old Testament.

Dating events in the Old Testament

In the last chapter, and indeed throughout this book, the dates given for the reigns of the kings of Israel, the Northern Kingdom of Israel and the Southern Kingdom of Judah are those that have been determined by Professor Edwin Thiele,[1] who, surprisingly, is relatively unknown. Yet this man achieved what no one before him had: from the data given in the Bible he established a detailed chronology for the kings of the Northern Kingdom of Israel and the Southern Kingdom of Judah in the Old Testament. This was no mean feat, for until Professor Thiele's achievement no one could make the numbers given for the lengths of the reigns of the kings of the Northern Kingdom of Israel agree with those given for the reigns of the kings of the Southern Kingdom of Judah. In fact, the chronology of the Hebrew kings formed part of Professor Thiele's doctoral programme at the University of Chicago. Until his monumental work, the dates that were established from the Bible seemed to be at variance with those established from the historical sources of the countries surrounding the land of Israel at the time. Basically, Professor Thiele accomplished two outstanding feats. Firstly, he established a single chronology for both the Northern Kingdom of Israel and the Southern Kingdom of Judah that got rid of all the apparent discrepancies that existed between the chronologies of these two kingdoms. And, secondly, he locked this chronology into the established chronologies fixed by modern astronomical records of the surrounding countries, notably those of Assyria and Babylon. Professor Thiele's work finally put all the pieces of the chronological jigsaw together for the period covering the reigns of the kings of the Northern Kingdom of Israel and the Southern Kingdom of Judah. It is no understatement to call this the work of a genius!

It will be good for us to understand how Professor Thiele achieved this. It must be stressed that Professor Thiele's prime assumption was that the chronologies found in the Old Testament are correct. The reason for this is that he was a Christian who believed that the Bible was the revealed word of God and therefore would be correct when referring to the history of God's people in the Old Testament. He argued that the chronologies of the Northern Kingdom of Israel and the Southern Kingdom of Judah must be capable of being harmonized, and that once harmonized, they would be in complete agreement with every fixed date in Middle Eastern history at which exact correspondence with Hebrew history could be established—for example, the date of the battle of Qarqar at which King Shalmaneser III of Assyria fought a coalition of a dozen nations including King Ahab of the Northern Kingdom of Israel;

and the date for the tribute payment by King Jehu of the Northern Kingdom of Israel to King Shalmaneser III of Assyria.

In order to untangle the Gordian knot[2] of the chronology of the Hebrew kings, Professor Thiele had to establish some basic historical dates. To do this, he consulted the Assyrian eponym list that covered every year in order from 892 BC to 648 BC. The Assyrians used to name each year in honour of a significant person within their government, and this person was known as the 'eponym' for that year. The historical events and documents in Assyria were then dated in terms of the eponym who held office for that year. Hence the eponym list provided a list of successive years in Assyrian history. From this list, Professor Thiele determined that a solar eclipse took place on 15 June 763 BC. Using this 'fixed' date, he showed that in 853 BC, King Shalmaneser III of Assyria fought a coalition of a dozen kings, including King Ahab of the Northern Kingdom of Israel, at the battle of Qarqar, an ancient town on the banks of the River Orontes in north-western Syria. The eponym list showed that twelve years later, in 841 BC, King Shalmaneser III of Assyria received tribute from King Jehu of the Northern Kingdom of Israel.[3] From this data and that given in the Bible, Professor Thiele then showed that King Ahab of the Northern Kingdom of Israel died in 853 BC and that Jehu acceded to the throne of the Northern Kingdom of Israel in 841 BC. This gave Professor Thiele a link with the absolute chronology of Assyria. Furthermore, he established another chronological link between the Bible and the absolute chronology of the Assyrian Empire from the eponym list: that King Sennacherib of Assyria invaded the Southern Kingdom of Judah at the time of King Hezekiah in 701 BC.

Turning his attention to the harmonization of the Hebrew kings, Professor Thiele studied the lengths of the reigns of the kings of the Northern Kingdom of Israel and of the Southern Kingdom of Judah given in the books of Kings and Chronicles. He came to the conclusion that the key to the solution for a harmonious chronology for the Hebrew kings is that these kingdoms did not use identical chronological methods. The first difference was the way they calculated the actual length of a particular king's reign; and the second one was the time of year they used to begin their regnal year.[4]

The Northern Kingdom of Israel used the 'Non-Accession Year System': the king began to reckon his first year from the day he first came to the throne. This meant that the portion of the final calendar year during which a king reigned was assigned to that king as his last year. As a result, the calendar year in question was assigned to two kings—the last year of the old king and the first year of the new king. Consequently, if a king was said to have ruled twelve years, then the actual length of his reign was only eleven years; and if five kings ruled for twelve years each, then the period covered by their reigns amounted to fifty-five years. Furthermore, if a king actually reigned for, say, two months, a month each side of the new year, he would be said to have reigned for two years!

On the other hand, the Southern Kingdom of Judah used the 'Accession Year System': when a king first came to the throne, the year was usually referred to as the king's accession year, but it was not until the first day of the first month of the first new calendar year that the king began reckoning events as his own first year. In this system, there was no duplication in the reckoning of years. If a king was said to have ruled twelve years, then twelve years was the length of his reign; and if five kings ruled for twelve years each, then the period covered by their reigns amounted to sixty years. However, if a king actually reigned for two months, a month each side of the new year, he would be said to have reigned for one year.

The consequence of this difference is that at the beginning, the Northern Kingdom of Israel appeared to be one year ahead of the Southern Kingdom of Judah, and for every new king it had, the time interval increased by one year. This resulted in an apparent difference between the absolute chronologies for these two kingdoms, and until

Professor Thiele realized the difference in the ways the Northern Kingdom of Israel and the Southern Kingdom of Judah calculated the lengths of the reigns of their kings, it was impossible to harmonize the different regnal years that were given in the Bible for the kings of the Northern Kingdom of Israel with those given for the kings of the Southern Kingdom of Judah. Understanding this difference solved the problem of harmonization.

Having looked at the first difference in the way the Northern Kingdom of Israel and the Southern Kingdom of Judah calculated the actual length of a particular king's reign, let us now turn our attention to the other chronological difference between them—the time of year they used to begin their regnal year. The Northern Kingdom of Israel and the Southern Kingdom of Judah did not begin their regnal years at the same time. The Northern Kingdom of Israel began its calendar year in Nisan (i.e. March/April) in the spring, and the Southern Kingdom of Judah reckoned its calendar year as beginning in Tishri (i.e. September/October) in the autumn. Hence for six months a year their years were in sync, and for six months a year they were out of sync.

To complicate matters even further, for a period of about sixty years beginning in the year of the reign of Queen Athaliah of the Southern Kingdom of Judah in 841 BC, the system that was used in the Northern Kingdom of Israel (that is, the Non-Accession Year System) was adopted by the Southern Kingdom of Judah, after which time the Southern Kingdom of Judah returned to its original system of reckoning.

There is yet a further complication, and that is the fact that there were a number of co-regencies and overlapping reigns. Although some of these are mentioned specifically in the historical books of the Old Testament, some have only been exposed by a careful study of the regnal data that is found in the Bible. A list of the co-regencies and rival reigns in the Northern Kingdom of Israel and the Southern Kingdom of Judah is given in Table 2.

TABLE 2: CO-REGENCIES AND RIVAL REIGNS IN THE NORTHERN KINGDOM OF ISRAEL AND SOUTHERN KINGDOM OF JUDAH[5]	
Kings	Cause
Northern Kingdom of Israel	
Omri and Tibni	Israel divided into two parts (1 Kings 16:21–22)
Jehoash and Jeroboam II	Imminent war (2 Kings 14:8–13; 2 Chr. 25:18–23)
Menahem and Pekah	Two nations in the north (Hosea 5:5)[6]
Southern Kingdom of Judah	
Asa and Jehoshaphat	Asa gravely ill (1 Kings 15:23; 2 Chr. 16:12)
Jehoshaphat and Jehoram	Imminent war (1 Kings 22:4, 32–33; noted in 2 Kings 8:16)
Amaziah and Azariah (Uzziah)	Amaziah captive in Israel (2 Kings 14:8–13, 21; 2 Chr. 25:21–24)
Azariah and Jotham	Leprosy of Azariah (2 Kings 15:5; 2 Chr. 26:21)
Jotham and Ahaz	Ahaz involved in pro-Assyrian coup (2 Kings 16:7)
Hezekiah and Manasseh	Illness of Hezekiah (2 Kings 20:1–6; 2 Chr. 32:24)

Although this explanation is lengthy and at times may be difficult to follow, it does give a rational explanation for the apparent discrepancies for the lengths of the reigns of the kings of the Northern Kingdom of Israel and of the Southern Kingdom of Judah that are recorded in the historical books of the Bible. We can see, therefore, that the events and time periods recorded in the books of Kings and Chronicles in the Old Testament are not at variance with each other and are not at variance with the events and chronologies recorded in the countries surrounding

Figure 1: The United Kingdom and the present area of Israel (including the
Golan Heights and Jerusalem) drawn to the same scale

the Northern Kingdom of Israel and the Southern Kingdom of Judah—chronologies which have been fixed by the dates on which eclipses took place, the dates of these eclipses having been confirmed by astronomical calculations. Once again we find that the events recorded in the Bible actually occurred and that the Bible is totally reliable, dependable and trustworthy, even in this area of chronology of the Northern Kingdom of Israel and the Southern Kingdom of Judah and the countries surrounding them.

The geography of Israel and its neighbours

One of the first problems we have in beginning to understand the geography of the countries mentioned in the Bible is realizing just how small the land occupied by the children of Israel actually was. Figure 1 on page 38 shows the United Kingdom and the present area of Israel (including the Golan Heights and Jerusalem) drawn to the same scale. To give some idea of how small the Southern Kingdom of Judah was, it was slightly smaller than North Wales without the Isle of Anglesey! Hence travelling around Israel did not take all that much time, even though people in Old Testament times were without modern forms of transportation and most had to rely on 'Shanks's pony' (i.e. they had to walk!).

The distances to other countries were, however, much further. Nineveh, the capital of the Assyrian Empire, was about 550 miles from Jerusalem as the crow flies—about 600 miles if you wanted to walk there avoiding the high mountains. Assuming you could walk about 20 miles a day for six days a week (having a day of rest on the Sabbath), it would take you five weeks to walk from Jerusalem to Nineveh. It is at this point that we should give a thought to Jonah, who was told by God to go (that is, take a five-week hike) to Nineveh and preach repentance to its citizens. Babylon was even further away—again 550 miles as the crow flies, but almost 700 miles following the route through the Fertile Crescent to avoid the high mountains. It would therefore take you almost six weeks[7] to walk there. This should give us an idea of the distance that the captives from the Southern Kingdom of Judah had to walk to their places of captivity in Babylonia and the distances involved in their return to the Promised Land. On the other hand, Egypt was on the doorstep, being 'only' 200 miles away from Jerusalem, taking just over a week and a half to walk there! Perhaps this will give us a fresh insight into the time it took for Joseph's brothers' journeys to and from Egypt to buy food, and also for the time it took Joseph, Mary and Jesus to travel to Egypt to escape Herod's wrath and his subsequent slaughter of the male babies and young children in Bethlehem and the surrounding areas.

The names of countries in the Old Testament are not always the same as the names we call them today. The most obvious examples of this are the empires of Assyria and Babylonia, which occupied the area that we now call Iraq. A good Bible atlas will be of great help in understanding where the countries mentioned in the Old Testament Scriptures were located, and it is good to refer to one when reading the historical accounts that are in the Old Testament.

Finally, the same problem occurs with the names of places. Although many villages and towns have the same names that they had three thousand years ago (e.g. Bethlehem and Jerusalem), some places have been renamed—an example being Joppa, the port which is now called Jaffa, from which the prophet Jonah departed for Tarshish. Other cities have disappeared and all that is left of them is a mound (e.g. Nineveh and Babylon). On the other hand, some towns and villages have been completely lost and we simply do not know *exactly* where these places were located—an example of this being Halah, a place in Assyria to which the Israelites were deported after the fall of Samaria in 723 BC (see 2 Kings 17:6).

Today, a country will often rename an important city for various reasons. Examples of this are the city of Mumbai in India, which until

1995 was known as Bombay, and the city of Harare, the capital of Zimbabwe, which until 1982 was known as Salisbury. Other countries build new capital cities. Examples of this are Brazil, which moved its capital from Rio de Janeiro to the newly built Brasilia in 1960, and Burma (now renamed Myanmar), which moved its capital from Rangoon to the newly built Naypyidaw in 2006. This is something which is not new, for we read in the Bible that at first the capital of the Northern Kingdom of Israel was Shechem, which King Jeroboam had built (see 1 Kings 12:25). Within thirty years, at the time of King Baasha, the capital was moved to Tirzah (1 Kings 15:33), and a few years later King Omri purchased the hill of Samaria and there started to build a new capital city, which he called Samaria (see 1 Kings 16:24). The building of the city of Samaria was completed by Omri's son, the infamous King Ahab.

Knowing this kind of information makes it a little easier to follow some of the stories recounted in the history books of the Old Testament and to understand better the history of the kings of the Northern Kingdom of Israel and the Southern Kingdom of Judah. For those wishing to know more about the geography of Israel and its neighbours, I heartily recommend the *ESV Bible Atlas* published in 2010 by Crossway. This atlas is very comprehensive and gives a detailed overview of the geography of the lands in the Middle East as well as lot of useful historical information about archaeological finds from these lands.

Israel, Judah, Samaria—who's who?

In later chapters of this book, we shall be looking in detail at the lives of Omri, Ahab and Jehu, who were kings of the Northern Kingdom of Israel, and also at the life of King Joash, who was a king of the Southern Kingdom of Judah. They lived in an extremely interesting period of history which lasted for eighty-nine years, beginning when Omri became king of the Northern Kingdom of Israel in 885 BC and ending when King Joash of the Southern Kingdom of Judah was murdered in 796 BC. This period is also of great interest for it gives the historical and political backgrounds to the ministries of those two great prophets of the Old Testament—Elijah and Elisha. We will also look at King Ahab's family connections. We will see that one of his daughters, Athaliah, became queen of the Southern Kingdom of Judah. We saw in the last chapter that understanding the relationship of the Northern Kingdom of Israel to the Southern Kingdom of Judah can be problematic when you read the historical books of the Old Testament, although keeping in mind the civil war in Israel that occurred when King Solomon died helps to distinguish between these two kingdoms. However, the Northern Kingdom of Israel is sometimes called Samaria, after its capital city—but not until Samaria was built during the reigns of King Omri and his son, King Ahab, some fifty to sixty years after the establishment of the Northern Kingdom of Israel under Jeroboam I. This can sometimes confuse things because the reader may not be aware of this nomenclature for the Northern Kingdom of Israel, or may confuse the kingdom of Samaria with the Samaritans. So how do we make sense of these names so that we can follow the history of what was going on at the time? In order to help, the next few paragraphs summarize the history of Israel that we looked at in the last chapter— from the time that the nation of Israel became a kingdom under its first king, Saul, in the eleventh century BC to the time of the fall of Jerusalem in 586 BC. This short overview will reinforce why we have these different names (Israel, Judah and Samaria) and to what kingdoms these names are referring. It will also help you better understand the overall history of the nation of Israel that is recorded in the Bible.

When Saul was made king of Israel, the nation of Israel was united—it is often referred to as the United Kingdom or the United Monarchy of Israel. Saul was succeeded by the famous King David, who reigned for a period of forty years, from 1010 to 970 BC, and he was succeeded by his son Solomon. At the death of Solomon in 930 BC there was a civil war in Israel that resulted in the United Kingdom of Israel being divided into two kingdoms—the Northern Kingdom of Israel in the north, and the Southern Kingdom of Judah in the south. The Southern Kingdom of Judah took its name from the largest tribe that occupied the southern area of the land of Israel, with Solomon's son Rehoboam ruling it from its capital, Jerusalem. The Northern Kingdom of Israel had its capital at Shechem and its first king was Jeroboam. The Northern Kingdom of Israel was, however, sometimes called Samaria after its new capital which, as we have already seen, was constructed in the reigns of King Omri and his son, King Ahab—they reigned from 885 to 853 BC.

In Hosea 5 (especially v. 5) there is a reference to Israel *and* Ephraim and they are referred to as two *separate* entities. It is thought that there were two kingdoms existing in the area occupied by the Northern Kingdom of Israel during the time when Hosea lived, which would explain why the entire book of Hosea reflects the existence of two kingdoms—Israel and Ephraim—in the north at this time. This would also explain the co-regency (shown in Table 2) of King Menahem and King Pekah in the Northern Kingdom of Israel in the mid-eighth century BC. However, this is not mentioned in either Kings or Chronicles. Therefore, Hosea's reference could be to the Northern Kingdom of Israel alone, giving it two names: that of Israel, its usual name, *and* that of the most important, influential and populous tribe in the Northern Kingdom of Israel—Ephraim.

The Northern Kingdom of Israel was defeated by the Assyrians and its capital Samaria fell in 723 BC, with the people taken into captivity. According to 2 Kings 17:6, the people from the Northern Kingdom of Israel were taken to three areas in the Assyrian Empire:

- Halah—in spite of much speculation, no one really knows *exactly* where this was;
- Habor/Gozan—the Khabur River, a tributary that flows south into the River Euphrates from the highlands of south-eastern Turkey and north-eastern Syria; and

- the cities of the Medes—south-western Iran.

These Israelites effectively disappeared and in spite of the many suggestions that have been put forward,[8] no one really knows what happened to them.

Over the next eighty years, the Assyrians brought in peoples from other countries that they had defeated to occupy the now semi-deserted Northern Kingdom of Israel. The peoples had different cultures, languages and religions from the Israelites and they were given the name Samaritans, derived from the word Samaria, a name given to the Northern Kingdom of Israel. The presence of the Samaritans in the land once occupied by the Northern Kingdom of Israel was resented by the people of the Southern Kingdom of Judah as well as by those from the Northern Kingdom of Israel who had not been taken into captivity. The origin of the Samaritans explains the attitude of the Jews towards the Samaritans which still existed at the time of the Lord Jesus Christ's ministry.

After the conquest of the Northern Kingdom of Israel by the Assyrians, the Southern Kingdom of Judah became even weaker, paying tribute to the Babylonians (who succeeded the Assyrians) in the hope that the Babylonians would allow them to remain in their land. However, the Babylonians invaded the Southern Kingdom of Judah at the end of the seventh century BC and Jerusalem was eventually captured and sacked on 10 July 586 BC. The people from the Southern Kingdom of Judah were taken into captivity in Babylon and began to return some seventy years later. The descendants of the people who returned from this exile were called the Jews. Strictly speaking, it is wrong to refer to any Israelite as a Jew before about 530 BC, for such nomenclature did not exist until then. The people who occupied the so-called Promised Land were Israelites. They were sometimes called Hebrews because of their being descended from Eber (hence Eberews—Hebrews) via Jacob, his father Isaac and his father Abraham. As Eber was the great-grandson of Shem, one of Noah's sons, the Israelites were also descended from Shem. Hence the Israelites and the Jews were Shemites or Semites, and this is how we get the term 'anti-Semitic'.

The names of kings

Reading the history recorded in the books of Kings and Chronicles in the Old Testament can be a daunting task. It is often difficult to follow many of the stories because sometimes the writer is referring to the Northern Kingdom of Israel and sometimes to the Southern Kingdom of Judah, but the reader is not always sure which. There are also problems with the names of the kings. For example, in the twelve-year period from 853 to 841 BC, we meet the following different kings who have the same names:

King Jehoram of **Judah**	The two reigned at the same time! (It is obvious that Jehoram is a variant spelling of Joram, and one was probably named after the other because of the close friendship at the time of the kings of the Southern Kingdom of Judah with those of the Northern Kingdom of Israel—see the family tree in Figure 3 on page 89.)
King Joram of **Israel**, who is also named Jehoram	
King Ahaziah of **Judah**, but who was also named Jehoahaz as well as Azariah	(This was probably due to the courtesy of the king of the Southern Kingdom of Judah and the king of the Northern Kingdom of Israel naming their heirs after each other!)
King Ahaziah of **Israel**	

Many of these names are unfamiliar to us today, and it is often difficult to remember exactly who a particular king was—especially when he is called one name in Kings and another in Chronicles! However, with perseverance it is possible to make sense of the stories that are recorded in the historical books of the Bible, especially with the help of family trees and the immensely useful book *The Mysterious Numbers of the Hebrew Kings* by Professor Thiele. It can also be very helpful to make your own notes and to construct your own family tree of the kings that you read about in the historical books in the Old Testament.

It cannot be overemphasized that the histories of the Southern Kingdom of Judah and the Northern Kingdom of Israel that are recorded in the Bible are not in any doubt, and anyone who says otherwise is speaking from a position of ignorance, not being aware of the enormous contribution that has been made in the last century by archaeological discoveries in the Middle East. The kings mentioned in the Old Testament—such as David, Omri, Ahab, Jehu, Jehoash, Jeroboam II, Menahem, Azariah, Ahaz, Pekah, Hoshea, Hezekiah and Manasseh—really existed and there is evidence for their existence from many extra-biblical sources. Those who claim that the Hebrew kings mentioned in the Bible did not exist are ignorant of the scholarly work that has been done on Old Testament history. For example, the work undertaken by such biblical scholars as Professor Edwin Thiele, who at the time of his retirement was Professor of Antiquity at Andrews University, Berrien Springs, Michigan, and Professor Alan Millard, who until his retirement was the Rankin Professor of Hebrew and Ancient Semitic Languages at the University of Liverpool, has shown that the biblical account of the history of Israel in the books of Kings and Chronicles can be trusted.[9]

The names of the kings of Assyria are even more unfamiliar to the English tongue. When you see a mother with her newborn child and you ask its name, you do not expect to get the answer, 'Oh, we have called him Sennacherib'! This name and those of the other Assyrian kings mentioned in the books of Kings and Chronicles are unfamiliar to us and we sometimes find them difficult to pronounce or remember. And as for their relationship to each other—well, let's be honest, most of us have not got a clue! The family tree of some of the kings of Assyria who are mentioned in the Bible and who are also referred to in this book is given in Figure 2 below. This family tree shows us clearly not only when these kings reigned but also their relationship with others.

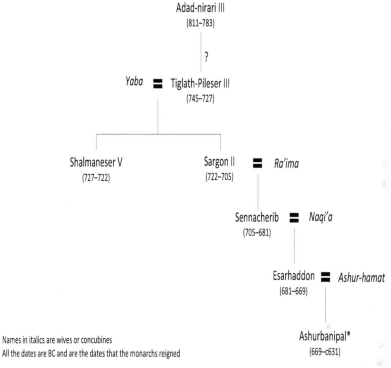

Names in italics are wives or concubines
All the dates are BC and are the dates that the monarchs reigned

* Called Asnappar or Osnappar in Ezra 4:10

Figure 2: The Royal Family tree of some of the Assyrian kings mentioned in this book

One particular Assyrian king deserves special mention as he had a great effect upon my life. This is Tiglath-Pileser III. He is mentioned a number of times in the Old Testament, and it is recorded in 1 Chronicles 5:26 that 'the God of Israel stirred up the spirit of Pul king of Assyria, and the spirit of Tilgath-pilneser king of Assyria, and he carried them [that is, some of the Northern Kingdom of Israel] away' (KJV). This text has often been used as proof that the Bible supports the position that Pul and Tiglath-Pileser III were two individual kings of Assyria. However, the Hebrew verb 'carried' is here in the singular and it is correctly translated with the singular pronoun 'he'. This conveys the idea that Pul and Tiglath-Pileser III were the same individual, and the correct translation of the *waw* introducing the phrase regarding Tiglath-Pileser should be 'even', as it is in all modern translations of the Scriptures. The fact that Pul is another name for Tiglath-Pileser III is borne out by the fact that Babylonian records have been discovered which show that his Babylonian name was Pulu and his Assyrian name was Tiglath-Pileser. The fact that Tiglath-Pileser and Pul were one and the same person and that he is referred to by both of his names in the Scriptures is further proof that the historical records of the Bible can be trusted. Indeed, it was this very fact that made me begin to realize the trustworthiness of the Bible, and this eventually led to my conversion.[10]

Summary and conclusion

In this chapter, we have looked at a number of problems that we encounter when we try to make sense of the history of Israel that is recounted in the Old Testament. We have seen that although there are no dates given in the narratives, we are able to determine the exact years of the reigns of the kings of the Northern Kingdom of Israel and the Southern Kingdom of Judah, thanks mainly to the work of Professor Edwin Thiele. The problem of the unfamiliarity of ancient Middle Eastern geography and place names can be readily solved using a good Bible atlas. We saw that time spent determining what or who constituted the United Kingdom of Israel, the Northern Kingdom of Israel, the Southern Kingdom of Judah, the Samaritans, the Jews, Samaria and Ephraim will greatly enrich our understanding of Old Testament history. Finally, light was shed on the difficulty of our unfamiliarity with the names of the kings mentioned in the Bible—both the kings of the Northern Kingdom of Israel and the Southern Kingdom of Judah, and those of Israel's neighbours and enemies, especially some of the Assyrian kings. I hope that we can now start to understand more fully the history that is recorded in the Old Testament.

NOTES

1 Edwin R. Thiele, *The Mysterious Numbers of the Hebrew Kings*, new rev. edn (Grand Rapids, MI: Kregel, 1994).

2 A 'Gordian knot' describes a difficult task and is named after an intricate knot tied by the king of Phrygia in ancient times. This knot remained tied until it was cut by Alexander the Great.

3 King Jehu of the Northern Kingdom of Israel is depicted paying tribute to Shalmaneser III on the so-called Black Obelisk of Shalmaneser, which is now located in the British Museum in London. See the section 'King Jehu in archaeology' in Chapter 5 for more details.

4 A regnal year is reckoned from the date or anniversary of a sovereign's accession.

5 Table taken from Thiele, *Mysterious Numbers of the Hebrew Kings*, p. 61.

6 Hosea 5:5 indicates that Ephraim and Israel were separate nations.

7 In Ezra 7:9 we read that it took Ezra and 'some of the people of Israel' (7:7, ESV) *four months* to walk from where they were being held in captivity in Babylonia (that is not the city of Babylon, but the area around it) to Jerusalem. This time period includes the time it took for the people to meet up with Ezra. Also a group of people would not have been able to walk 20 miles a day as part of the day would have been taken up with finding food and cooking it for the group.

8 One of the most intriguing of these is that they migrated across Europe as Celts, Angles and Saxons, eventually settling in north-west Europe and the British Isles.

9 See Thiele, *Mysterious Numbers of the Hebrew Kings*; and Alan Millard, *Discoveries from Biblical Times* (Oxford: Lion, 1997).

10 A more detailed discussion of the evidence for Pul and Tiglath-Pileser being the same individual can be found in Thiele, *Mysterious Numbers of the Hebrew Kings*, pp. 139–141.

King Omri of the Northern Kingdom of Israel

If we were to rely solely on the Bible for our knowledge about King Omri of the Northern Kingdom of Israel, we would know very little about him, for the Bible devotes only eight verses of Scripture to him and his reign, namely, 1 Kings 16:21–28. Two of these verses are devoted to how Omri came to power; one gives details about the length of his reign; one verse describes his building of the new capital city of Samaria; two verses explain how evil he was; one verse gives details of where other records about King Omri's reign could be found at the time when the first book of Kings was being written; and one verse gives details of where King Omri was buried and the fact that his son, Ahab, succeeded him as king. In addition to these eight verses, there is also a reference in 1 Kings 20:34 to the king of Aram having captured cities from King Omri and also having set up markets in Samaria.

I have given this book the title *Rogues in Royal Robes* for I am of the opinion that people like Omri were in fact rogues. All we know about Omri's background is that he was the commander of the army (1 Kings 16:16). In fact, he may not have been an Israelite at all, for the Bible does not give any details of his ancestry—we do not know the name of his father or any of his genealogical details. Furthermore, W. Thiel has suggested[1] that Omri's name might be either Amorite or Arabic,[2] suggesting that he was a foreign mercenary. Also, because King Omri's son Ahab married the Phoenician princess Jezebel, it has even been suggested that Omri himself was a Phoenician.[3]

In spite of the fact that the Bible devotes so few verses to King Omri, this king was given an elevated position in the Assyrian records of the day. Whenever the Assyrians referred to the Northern Kingdom of Israel, they always referred to it as *Bit-Humri*, which means 'the House of Omri',[4] and its capital, Samaria, as *Beth-Khumri*, which means 'the house or palace of Omri'.[5] In other words, they did not refer to it by the name of *Israel*, but by the name of *Omri*. Furthermore, it was customary on Assyrian royal inscriptions to refer to a royal dynasty by its founder, and so, for example, on the Black Obelisk of Shalmaneser III which is located in the British Museum in London, King Jehu of the Northern Kingdom of Israel is referred to as a 'son of Omri' even though he was, in fact, unrelated to King Omri and had killed all of his descendants.

One of the most visited items in the British Museum is the Rosetta Stone. On this stone there is a citation to celebrate the first anniversary of Pharaoh Ptolemy V in 195 BC. The citation is in three languages and is identical. It is in Egyptian hieroglyphics (used by the priests), in demotic Egyptian (used by ordinary people) and in Greek capital letters (the language of administration). At the time of its discovery in 1799, no one could read the first two texts. A full translation of the Greek text was published in 1803, but it was almost twenty years before a transliteration of the Egyptian scripts was announced in 1822 and it took longer still before scholars were able to read the Ancient Egyptian inscriptions and literature confidently. Because of the popularity of the Rosetta Stone, Jean-François Champollion is well known as the first scholar to successfully have deciphered hieroglyphics before his death in 1832.

However, most of the inscriptions that were recorded by the Assyrians and which refer to contemporary biblical characters and events are in cuneiform, a script that dates back to about 3000 BC. It has about three hundred signs and was the common script across the so-called Fertile Crescent until the alphabet replaced it in about 1000 BC. The story surrounding the deciphering of cuneiform script is not as well known as the story of the deciphering of hieroglyphics, probably because the trilingual stone monument that was used to crack cuneiform script is not in any museum but is found on a rockface some 15 metres (about 50 feet) high by 25 metres (about 80 feet) wide and located 100 metres (about 330 feet) up a limestone cliff at Mount Behistun in Kermanshah Province near the city of Kermanshah in western Iran. It was designated a UNESCO World Heritage Site in 2006. The carvings on the Behistun Rock were carved between 522 BC and 486 BC and show King Darius the Great of Persia. Like the Rosetta Stone, the text is in three languages—but in this case, all three languages are cuneiform: Old Persian, Elamite and Babylonian (Akkadian). In 1835 Sir Henry Rawlinson, an officer in the British East India Company, climbed the rock and perched precariously on a ledge half a metre (about 20 inches) wide above a sheer drop of 100 metres (about 330 feet) and, with the aid of ladders from below and swings from above, copied the Behistun inscriptions using papier mâché squeezed into the script; by 1846 he was able to decipher cuneiform script. It is because scholars can read cuneiform script that we know so much about the history of Assyria and Babylonia, and also about the history of the Northern Kingdom of Israel that is not recorded in the Scriptures.

The historical background to Omri's becoming king of the Northern Kingdom of Israel

As we saw in Chapter 1, the kingship in the Northern Kingdom of Israel was not always handed down from father to son—it was often gained by murdering not only the reigning king, but also all his offspring and other members of his family. This is what Omri did in order to become king of the Northern Kingdom of Israel, and it will be helpful for us to examine exactly how he achieved this. We have seen that following the civil war in Israel after King Solomon had died in 930 BC, Jeroboam I was the first king of the Northern Kingdom of Israel. He was an evil king and set up two golden calves—one in Dan in the north of the country and the other in Bethel in the south. He then told the people the fake news that these were the gods that had brought them out of the land of Egypt. Can you imagine anything so deceitful? Only a few hundred years had passed since the Lord had led his people out of Egypt, and here was the king telling them that it was these two golden idols that had done so. No wonder the Bible used him as an illustration of, and a yardstick and byword for, evil in the early chapters of the books of Kings and Chronicles.

Now let us look in detail at how Omri became king of the Northern Kingdom of Israel. According to 1 Kings 14:20, Jeroboam I reigned for twenty-two years, but because of the way the Hebrews calculated the lengths of reigns in the Northern Kingdom of Israel,[6] his actual reign was twenty-one years—from 930 to 909 BC. King Jeroboam I was succeeded by his son, Nadab, who was also an evil king and who, according to 1 Kings 15:25, reigned for two years—one actual year—from 909 to 908 BC. King Nadab was assassinated by Baasha, who the Bible informs us was 'the son of Ahijah, of the house of Issachar' (1 Kings 15:27, NKJV). This assassination occurred at Gibbethon[7] in the territory of Dan while King Nadab and his army were besieging this city in an attempt to win it back from the Philistines who had captured it. Baasha set himself up as king of the Northern Kingdom of Israel and established himself in this position by killing 'all the house of Jeroboam' (1 Kings 15:29, NKJV). In other words, he murdered anyone who had a legitimate claim to be king by virtue of being descended from Jeroboam I (remember that King Nadab, whom Baasha had assassinated, was Jeroboam's son). According to 1 Kings 15:34, King Baasha was also an evil king, for 'he did evil in the sight of the LORD' (NKJV). He reigned for twenty-four years (1 Kings 15:33)—twenty-three actual years—from 908 to 886 BC.[8]

Through the prophet Jehu, the son of Hanani, the Lord promised that the house of Baasha would be removed from reigning over God's people (see 1 Kings 16:1–4), and it was not long before King Baasha died and his son Elah gained the throne. However, it turned out that King Elah was a drunkard, and this was his downfall. The Bible records that Elah went to the house of Arza in Tirzah, which at that time was the capital city of the

Northern Kingdom of Israel, and that Elah drank until he was drunk. Zimri, who was one of Elah's servants and commander of half the king's chariots, took advantage of this and murdered King Elah, who had reigned only two years (1 Kings 16:8)—that is, only one actual year—from 886 to 885 BC. Zimri took no time in establishing himself as king. In 1 Kings 16:11 we are informed that 'as soon as he [i.e. Zimri] was seated on his throne . . . he killed all the household of Baasha; he did not leave him one male, neither of his relatives nor of his friends' (NKJV). He must have undertaken this task very quickly, for he reigned only seven days! As noted earlier, Prime Minister Harold Wilson declared that 'a week is a long time in politics'.

While these events were going on in Tirzah, the army of the Northern Kingdom of Israel was once again besieging Gibbethon, trying to wrest it from the Philistines. However, when they heard the news of Elah's assassination by Zimri, they made Omri, the commander of the army, their king. Immediately Omri took his army to Tirzah and besieged the city. When King Zimri saw the Israelite army capturing the city, he committed suicide by setting fire to and destroying the king's palace while he was inside it (see 1 Kings 16:17–19).

King Omri should have started reigning over the Northern Kingdom of Israel immediately, but Tibni the son of Ginath also claimed the kingship. As a result, the people of the Northern Kingdom of Israel 'were divided into two parts: half of the people followed Tibni the son of Ginath, to make him king, and half followed Omri' (1 Kings 16:21, NKJV). This rivalry lasted for five years,[9] from 885 to 880 BC, after which time 'the people who followed Omri prevailed over the people who followed Tibni the son of Ginath. So Tibni died and Omri reigned' (1 Kings 16:22, NKJV). Thus Omri became king of the Northern Kingdom of Israel in what can only be described as troublesome times, and he reigned as the sole king over the Northern Kingdom of Israel for a period of seven years, from 880 to 873 BC.

In 1 Kings 16:25 it is recorded that 'Omri did evil in the eyes of the LORD and sinned more than all those before him' (NIV). Yet, as we shall see in the next chapter when we study the life of Omri's son, King Ahab was even more evil than his father King Omri, and God raised up Jehu (whom we shall look at in more detail in Chapter 5) to make sure that none of Ahab's descendants (and therefore none of Omri's descendants) ruled over the Northern Kingdom of Israel. The reason why King Omri is given so little space in the biblical records of the history of the Northern Kingdom of Israel is that biblical history is written from God's point of view, and in God's eyes King Omri was so evil it was not worth going into detail about his exploits. That is why we know so little about him.

Establishing Samaria as the capital of the Northern Kingdom of Israel

The first capital of the Northern Kingdom of Israel was Shechem, a city located in the hill country of Ephraim north of Bethel and Shiloh on the high road going from Jerusalem to the northern districts. It was the town where Solomon's son Rehoboam met with all Israel and it is where the tribes from what became the Northern Kingdom of Israel rebelled against Rehoboam when he refused to meet their demands to make their burdens lighter. As a result, they made Jeroboam their king and Shechem their capital. This took place almost three thousand years ago, in 930 BC. Shechem had had a remarkable history and as such was a good choice for a capital. About a thousand years earlier, the Lord had appeared to Abraham at Shechem and had told him that he was going to give that country to Abraham's descendants (Gen. 12:6–7). The Israelites who had carried the body of Joseph with them out of Egypt buried it at Shechem (Josh. 24:32). Today the ruins of the ancient city of Shechem, known in Arabic as Tell el-Balata, lie just over a mile south-east of the modern Arab city of Nablus on the northern West Bank.

King Jeroboam I of the Northern Kingdom of Israel did not keep

Shechem as his capital for very long; he soon vacated it, fortified the town of Penuel and made that city his capital instead. King Jeroboam I rebuilt Penuel as his second capital, perhaps to better administer his domains beyond the Jordan River. Although the exact site of Penuel is unknown today, it has been associated with the beautiful ruins of the eastern mound at Tulul al-Dhahab (now called the Golden Hill on the Zarqa River [also known as the Yabbok River] in Jordan). Penuel is also called Peniel in the Bible and is where Jacob received his new name of Israel after wrestling face to face with God all night. Jacob called the place Peniel because in Hebrew 'Peniel' sounds like 'the face of God'.

The city of Tirzah in the territory of Manasseh became the third capital city of the Northern Kingdom of Israel in the time of Jeroboam I. When Baasha assassinated Jeroboam's son and successor, Nadab, and became king of the Northern Kingdom of Israel, King Baasha ruled from his palace in the capital in Tirzah for twenty-three years. He was succeeded by his son Elah, who reigned for a year before being assassinated by the usurper King Zimri, who reigned for a week in Tirzah before being burned alive in the palace during his rival Omri's conquest of the city. Once King Omri's five-year dispute with Tibni was over and he had established himself as king of the Northern Kingdom of Israel, he reigned from Tirzah for six years before transferring his capital to the newly built city of Samaria. Tirzah was very likely destroyed along with the city of Samaria by the Assyrians in 723 BC.

Samaria was the last capital city of the Northern Kingdom of Israel. It was named after Shemer who sold his hill to King Omri of the Northern Kingdom of Israel in about 880 BC for two silver talents.[10] The hill was situated on an isolated elevation some 300 feet (about 90 metres) high (and so was easy to defend) around 7 miles (11 km) north of Shechem, and the site featured a rectangular flattened top on which Omri built his capital. King Omri, and his son King Ahab, built royal palaces into its walls and an ivory house for Ahab's infamous Phoenician consort Queen

Jezebel, and here King Ahab met with King Jehoshaphat of the Southern Kingdom of Judah. Samaria was the capital of the Northern Kingdom of Israel for almost 160 years, until it fell to the invading Assyrians in 723 BC.

The sacking of the city of Samaria by the Assyrian army in 723 BC

The Bible tells us in 2 Kings 17:5 that King Shalmaneser V invaded the Northern Kingdom of Israel and besieged the city of Samaria for three years before it fell. Professor Edwin Thiele has shown[11] that the first destruction of Samaria by the Assyrians took place in 723 BC during the reign of Shalmaneser V, who reigned from 727 to 722 BC. But Sargon II, who reigned from 722 to 705 BC, claimed that he took Samaria, and as a result, 722 BC came to be looked upon as the date of Samaria's fall. This date is found in almost all commentaries, encyclopaedias and textbooks that record the date of the fall of Samaria. Professor Thiele has pointed out that a number of outstanding scholars have carefully studied this subject and definitely concluded that Samaria fell in 723 BC; hence this is the date that I have consistently used in this book.

The invasion of the Northern Kingdom of Israel by the Assyrians must have brought terror into the hearts of God's people, especially those who were living in its capital. Assyria was probably the first military power in history and its army was composed of over three hundred thousand well-trained, fit and skilful soldiers who were well equipped and who were led by brilliant generals who used imaginative strategies and tactics to defeat Assyria's enemies and expand its territory. The army was composed of chariots, cavalry and infantry and it also used effective siege engines and battering rams to break down walls over which its troops, using ladders, could then climb and enter the besieged town or city. The chariots used by the Assyrian army had a solid platform on which were two soldiers: one controlled the two or three horses that pulled it; the other fought the enemy using a bow and arrows. The platform of the chariot was supported by two, or sometimes four, wheels that had metal tyres made of copper, bronze or iron. The Assyrian cavalrymen wore light armour and carried weapons such as 5-foot-long metal-pointed wooden spears, javelins and daggers as well as bows and arrows with iron heads. The infantry was composed of soldiers armed with shields, swords, spears, javelins, daggers, bows and arrows, and slings. These slings were not children's slings but could project smooth stones the size of tennis balls at 100–150 mph (about 160–250 kph) which could seriously injure or even kill. The siege engines consisted of a tank-like wooden structure which ran along on four or six wheels. On top of this was a small wooden tower from which archers provided covering fire as the whole machine was pushed forward, usually up an earthen ramp that had been built by the Assyrian troops and which reached right up to the walls that were to be attacked. The archers on the siege engine together with the whole structure were kept doused with water in order to extinguish any flaming torches thrown by the enemy from the tops of the walls that were under attack. A very large long log with a metal tip was then placed at the front of this formidable siege engine in order to attack the walls of the town or city that was being besieged. The walls were not made of stone but of clay and so could easily be destroyed by this very effective battering ram, which actually destroyed the walls by gradually picking away at them, causing them to collapse, rather than by battering them down.

A captured city was usually plundered and burnt to the ground, and its site was deliberately denuded by killing its trees. The loyalty of the troops was secured by dividing a large part of the spoils among them . . . Soldiers were rewarded for every severed head they brought in from the field, so that the aftermath of a victory generally witnessed the wholesale decapitation of fallen foes. Most often the prisoners . . . were dispatched after the battle; they knelt with their backs to their captors, who beat their heads in with clubs, or cut them off with cutlasses. Scribes stood by to count the number of prisoners taken and killed by each soldier, and apportioned the booty accordingly; the king, if time permitted, presided at the slaughter . . . The nobles among the defeated were given more special treatment: their ears, noses, hands and feet were sliced off, or they were thrown from high towers, or they and their children were beheaded, or flayed alive or roasted over a slow fire.[12]

The savagery and brutality displayed by the Assyrian army knew no bounds. The leaders of the enemy were usually publicly humiliated in victory parades before being disembowelled, flayed alive, impaled or mutilated in one way or another. Sometimes the tongues of prisoners were cut off before they were executed by being flayed alive. At other times the eyes of prisoners were gouged out with lances while their heads were held in place with a cord passing through their lips. After the victorious battles Assyrian soldiers, accompanied by musicians, often played catch with the severed heads of their enemies. Such violence against the defeated foe was justified by the Assyrians who saw it as divine retribution for those who had rebelled against the king of Assyria and his gods.

We know how cruel the Assyrians were not only from their own writings, but also from the carved stone reliefs that King Sennacherib made of his army's attack on the town of Lachish in 701 BC and which he erected in his palace in his capital, Nineveh. These Lachish reliefs now reside in the British Museum in London and are well worth visiting to see how the Assyrian army attacked and subdued their enemies.

The siege of Lachish . . . began, as such military contests often did, with Assyrian envoys riding up to the city walls to demand surrender. The people were told that, if they complied, they would be treated well while, if they resisted, they would suffer the common fate of all who had resisted before them. Even though it was well known that the Assyrians showed no mercy, the defenders of Lachish chose to take their chances and hold their city.[13]

The envoys returned to the Assyrian encampment and the siege of Lachish commenced.

Using the carved stone reliefs depicting the siege of Lachish by the Assyrians, Dr Simon Anglim, a military historian at the Department of War Studies at King's College, London, has described the siege of Lachish as follows:

The city was first surrounded to prevent escape. Next, archers were brought forward; under the cover of giant shields, they cleared the battlements. The king then used the tried-and-tested Assyrian method of building an earthen ramp close to the enemy wall, covering it with flat stone and wheeling forward a machine that combined a siege-tower with a battering ram. The Assyrians then staged a two-pronged assault. The tower was wheeled up the ramp and the ram was brought to bear against the mid-section of the enemy wall. Archers in the tower cleared the battlements while bowmen on the ground pushed up close to the wall to cover an infantry assault with scaling ladders. The fighting appears to have been intense, and the assault probably took several days, yet eventually the Assyrians entered the city. Archaeology has revealed that the place was looted and hundreds of men, women, and children were put to the sword. The relief of the siege [at Nineveh] shows prisoners begging for mercy at the feet of Sennacherib. Others less fortunate, perhaps the city's leaders, have been impaled upon stakes.[14]

No wonder the people of the Northern Kingdom of Israel dreaded King Shalmaneser V and his army invading their land and attacking the city of Samaria. The above paragraph describes the horrors of the Assyrians attacking and laying siege to a small town just for a few days. Imagine what it would have been like for the inhabitants of the large capital city of Samaria to have been besieged by the Assyrians for three years, and then for them to be taken prisoner, for their nobles and leaders to be executed and for their women and children to be killed in the cruel ways described above. It does not bear thinking about.

Who were the Samaritans?

Even non-Christians are familiar with the term 'the Good Samaritan', a term that has come to mean a person who selflessly helps others, especially those in distress. It is taken from one of Jesus' parables: the Good Samaritan was the only person who stopped and helped a Jewish man who had been robbed and beaten and who had been 'passed by' and ignored by a Jewish priest and a Jewish Levite who did not want to help in case, by getting involved, they became ceremonially unclean. In Jesus' parable, a Samaritan came along and it was he who helped the Jew who had been beaten and robbed. Not only did the Good Samaritan care for the Jew medically, but he also used his own transport (his donkey) and took him to the local inn, paying for him to stay there until he was fully recovered. Those are the bare bones of the parable of the Good Samaritan. But there was a lot more going on, as we shall see.

I am convinced that most Christians have no idea who the Samaritans of our Lord's day were. In fact, Christians would be hard pressed to give a meaningful account of the ancestry of the Samaritans and explain why there was so much animosity between them and the Jews at the time of Christ. And there was a great deal of animosity, for we read in John 4:9 that at the time of Christ the Jews and the Samaritans did not even share the same dishes! Furthermore, the parable of the Good Samaritan was given by Jesus in response to a question asked by an expert in the Law about who his neighbour was. At the end of the parable Jesus asked this expert in the Law who he thought had been the neighbour to the man who had been robbed. The simple answer was, of course, the Samaritan. It could not be plainer. Furthermore, the Jews and the Samaritans actually lived side by side in the same land! They were neighbours! But the expert in the Law could not bring himself to utter this, saying instead, 'The one who had mercy on him' (Luke 10:37, NIV). It is only when we realize the hatred that the Jews had for the Samaritans that we fully appreciate the impact that this parable must have had on its hearers when they first heard it.

So who were the Samaritans? Where did they come from? Why did the Jews hate them so much? As we saw in Chapter 2, the Samaritans are named after Samaria, which, as we have seen, was the name of the last capital city of the Northern Kingdom of Israel, and also the name by which the Northern Kingdom of Israel was known. After the Assyrians had defeated the Northern Kingdom of Israel and sacked its capital in 723 BC, and had taken people from the Northern Kingdom of Israel captive into the Assyrian Empire, they repopulated the cities of the Northern Kingdom of Israel with people from the cities of Babylon, Cuth, Ivvah, Hamath and Sepharvaim. The land of the Northern Kingdom of Israel was therefore repopulated with foreign people, and it was the descendants of these people who were the Samaritans of the Lord Jesus Christ's time. A look at any map of the time will show that some of these people were moved several hundred miles from where they originally lived. This deportation of large segments of the population was standard policy in the Assyrian Empire as it was seen to be the best way to prevent any rebellions and conflicts—remove the former occupants of the land and replace them with Assyrians. This depopulation and repopulation of the Northern Kingdom of Israel was carried out by the Assyrian kings Sargon II, Esarhaddon and Ashurbanipal, and Scripture references to them are found in 2 Kings 17:5–6, 24 and Ezra 4:1–2, 9–10.

One historian writes that

the deportees, their labour and their abilities were extremely valuable to the Assyrian state, and their relocation was carefully planned and organised. We must not imagine treks of destitute fugitives who were easy prey for famine and disease: the deportees were meant to travel as comfortably and safely as possible in order to reach their destination in good physical shape. Whenever deportations are depicted in Assyrian imperial art, men, women and children are shown travelling in groups, often riding on vehicles or animals and never in bonds. There is no reason to doubt these depictions as Assyrian narrative art does not otherwise shy away from the graphic display of extreme violence [as, for example, on the carved stone reliefs depicting the siege of Lachish, as we saw above].[15]

Also,

Deportees were carefully chosen for their abilities and sent to regions which could make the most of their talents. Not everyone in the conquered populace was chosen for deportation and families were never separated. Those segments of the population that had actively resisted the Assyrians were killed or sold into slavery, but the general populace became absorbed into the growing empire and were thought of as Assyrians.[16]

Summary and conclusion

We have seen that we know very little about King Omri from the Scriptures as there are only eight verses written about him. We know much more about him and his exploits from Assyrian cuneiform script. We know that the Assyrians called the Northern Kingdom of Israel the land of Omri after him, such was the high regard in which they held him. King Omri was instrumental in establishing Samaria as the capital city of the Northern Kingdom of Israel. When Samaria was sacked by the Assyrian army in 723 BC, the Assyrians deported the Israelites living in the Northern Kingdom of Israel and repopulated the empty cities with foreign peoples, whose descendants were the Samaritans of the Lord Jesus Christ's time.

Even though we are only halfway through this book, it cannot be overemphasized that as a result of the wickedness of the rogues in royal robes who ruled the Northern Kingdom of Israel, the Lord was very angry with his people. This is summarized in what is perhaps one of the saddest passages in the Scriptures:

Samaria [that is, the Northern Kingdom of Israel] fell because the Israelites sinned against the LORD their God, who had rescued them from the king of Egypt and had led them out of Egypt. They worshiped other gods, followed the customs of the people whom the LORD had driven out as his people advanced, and adopted customs introduced by the kings of Israel. The Israelites did things that the LORD their God disapproved of. They built pagan places of worship in all their towns, from their smallest village to the largest city. On all the hills and under every shady tree they put up stone pillars and images of the goddess Asherah, and they burned incense on all the pagan altars, following the practice of the people whom the LORD had driven out of the land. They aroused the LORD's anger with all their wicked deeds and disobeyed the LORD's command not to worship idols.

The LORD had sent his messengers and prophets to warn Israel and Judah: 'Abandon your evil ways and obey my commands, which are contained in the Law I gave to your ancestors and which I handed on to you through my servants the prophets.' But they would not obey; they were stubborn like their ancestors, who had not trusted in the LORD their God. They refused to obey his instructions, they did not keep the covenant he had made with their ancestors, and they disregarded his warnings. They worshiped worthless idols and became worthless themselves, and they followed the customs of the surrounding nations, disobeying the LORD's command not to imitate them. They broke all the laws of the LORD their God and made two metal bull-calves to worship; they also made an image of the goddess Asherah, worshiped the stars, and served the god Baal. They sacrificed their sons and daughters as burnt offerings to pagan gods; they consulted mediums and fortunetellers, and they devoted themselves completely to doing what is wrong in the LORD's sight, and so aroused his anger. The LORD was angry with the Israelites and banished them from his sight, leaving only the kingdom of Judah. (2 Kings 17:7–18, GNT)

The Southern Kingdom of Judah did not learn from the mistakes that their brothers and sisters had made in the Northern Kingdom of Israel and they, too, in general, also had rogues for their kings. With one or two exceptions, these kings led them astray, and eventually the people of the

Chapter 3

Southern Kingdom of Judah were taken captive into Babylon. However, there is one king who was not, and is not, a rogue, and we shall be looking at him in the last chapter of this book. He is, of course, the Lord Jesus Christ, the King of kings; he sits on the royal throne of David, and of his kingdom there shall be no end.

NOTES

1 W. Thiel, in *The Anchor Bible Dictionary*, vol. 5 (New York: Doubleday, 1992), p. 17.

2 The Israelites having an Arab as their king is a very thought-provoking idea given the political situation that exists in the Middle East in the twenty-first century!

3 Jeffrey K. Kuan, 'Was Omri a Phoenician?', in M. Patrick Graham et al. (eds.), *History and Interpretation: Essays in Honour of John H. Hayes*, Journal for the Study of the Old Testament Supplement Series 173 (Sheffield: Sheffield Academic Press, 1993), pp. 232–233.

4 Karen Radner, 'Israel, the "House of Omri"', *Assyrian Empire Builders*, University College London, 2012, https://www.ucl.ac.uk/sargon/essentials/countries/israel/.

5 See 'Samaria (Ancient City)', Wikipedia, https://en.wikipedia.org/wiki/Samaria_(ancient_city).

6 In the Northern Kingdom of Israel the Non-Accession Method of measuring the length of a king's reign was used. This is explained in the section 'Dating events in the Old Testament' in Chapter 2. The result is that the kings in the Northern Kingdom of Israel actually reigned for one year less than the time stated in the Bible.

7 Gibbethon is probably modern Tell el-Melat, west of Gezer, according to *The New Bible Dictionary* (London: IVP, 1970), p. 466.

8 It is common practice in more academic studies to give the two Julian years that contain the date in question—hence the date of the death of King Baasha should be 886/5 BC. However, to simplify things, the author has given a single year for the date of the beginning and end of the reigns of the kings, but this means that the length of the reign does not always compute correctly.

9 The length of this rivalry has been determined by Edwin R. Thiele, *The Mysterious Numbers of the Hebrew Kings*, new rev. ed (Grand Rapids, MI: Kregel, 1994), p. 88.

10 This is worth about £27,500 in today's money (as at March 2020).

11 Thiele, *Mysterious Numbers of the Hebrew Kings*, pp. 137–138, 163–172.

12 Will Durant, *Our Oriental Heritage*, vol. 1 (New York: Simon and Schuster, 1963), pp. 271, 275–276.

13 Joshua J. Mark, 'Assyrian Warfare', Ancient History Encyclopedia, last modified 2 May 2018, https://www.ancient.eu/Assyrian_Warfare/.

14 S. Anglim et al., *Fighting Techniques of the Ancient World 3000 BC–AD 500* (London: Amber Books, 2013), p. 190.

15 Karen Radner, cited by Mark, 'Assyrian Warfare'.

16 Mark, 'Assyrian Warfare'.

King Ahab of the Northern Kingdom of Israel

When King Omri of the Northern Kingdom of Israel died, he was buried in the capital city of Samaria, and his son, Ahab, succeeded him and reigned for twenty-two years—that is, twenty-one actual years, from 874 to 853 BC—as king of the Northern Kingdom of Israel (1 Kings 16:28–29). We saw in the previous chapter that a mere eight verses of the Bible are allocated to the life and times of King Omri. However, in stark contrast, almost four chapters of the Bible (1 Kings 18; 20; 21; 22) are dedicated to giving an account of the life and times of his son, King Ahab—this is more than is assigned to any other king of the Northern Kingdom of Israel. However, as we shall see, these chapters are nothing more than a catalogue of the bad behaviour and the unlawful acts committed against the Lord by King Ahab and his evil wife, Jezebel.

One of the unlawful acts carried out by King Ahab and his wife, Jezebel, was the sinful act of gaining possession of Naboth's vineyard. This was pivotal in the life of King Ahab and it had unforeseen consequences, as we shall see. King Ahab not only had a palace in the capital city of Samaria but he also established one in the city of Jezreel, which is about 21 miles (about 35 km) north of Samaria. Next to the king's palace in Jezreel was a fine vineyard which was owned by Naboth and which King Ahab tried to purchase so he could use it as a vegetable garden. Now, the Law of Moses did not allow Naboth to sell the vineyard, not even to the king. However, Jezebel managed to obtain Naboth's vineyard for her husband by arranging for Naboth to be murdered. The unforeseen consequence of the acquisition of Naboth's vineyard through

Jezebel's conniving was that King Ahab's entire family was condemned to death by the prophet Elijah (1 Kings 21:17–29). King Ahab lost his life in a battle against the Syrians at Ramoth Gilead and he was buried in Samaria; the rest of his family were killed by Jehu, as we shall see in the next chapter.

King Ahab and archaeology

It is a common myth that there is no archaeological evidence for the existence of King Ahab of the Northern Kingdom of Israel or of the events of his life that we read about in the books of Kings and Chronicles. In order to believe this myth we would have to dismiss the biblical accounts of King Ahab's mighty army, his palace decorated with ivory that he built in the capital city of Samaria (his so-called 'ivory house', 1 Kings 22:39, ESV) and all the cities that he built or extensively rebuilt in his kingdom. We would also have to reject the biblical account surrounding the aftermath of his death. However, in the light of discoveries made by archaeologists about the life and times of King Ahab, this myth has to be firmly rejected and thrown into the rubbish bin where it belongs.

The first archaeological discovery to examine is an account of a battle that is not mentioned in the Bible but is described on the Kurkh monolith of Shalmaneser III, which now resides in the British Museum in London. This stone pillar was discovered in 1861 on the banks of the River Tigris at Kurkh in south-eastern Turkey by the amateur British archaeologist John George Taylor, who at the time was an agent of the British East India Company and an official of the Foreign Office working as the British Consul-General for Kurdistan. The stone monolith is just over 7 feet (2.2 m) tall, 34 inches (87 cm) wide and 9 inches (23 cm) thick. On the front of this stone pillar is a huge relief of King Shalmaneser III of Assyria, and the whole of the monolith, both front and back, is covered with cuneiform script which gives an account of the battles fought by this king. Of particular significance is the description of his victory in the sixth year of his reign, in 853 BC, over a coalition of a dozen kings at the battle of Qarqar, an ancient town on the banks of the River Orontes in north-western Syria. The cuneiform inscription states that this coalition was led by King Benhadad of Damascus and included King Ahab of the Northern Kingdom of Israel. The writing states that King Ahab's army was composed of two thousand chariots and ten thousand infantry, which reveals the strength of King Ahab's kingdom at the time. Interestingly, the inscription on the Kurkh monolith is one of the earliest explicit references to Israel that has been discovered, although other such early allusions may be found in the future. Such inscriptions as that found on this stone pillar again reveal that the Northern Kingdom of Israel was not some mythical kingdom in a far-away land but that it actually existed and that the Bible accurately records the name of the king (Ahab) who ruled over it in the middle of the ninth century BC. It also shows that the Bible accurately records the names of the countries around the Northern Kingdom of Israel, together with the names of their rulers who existed at the time.

In addition to the evidence for the existence of King Ahab furnished by the Kurkh monolith, evidence also comes from excavations made at the ancient city of Samaria where King Ahab lived. In Chapter 3, when discussing the establishment of Samaria as the capital of the Northern Kingdom of Israel, we saw that King Omri, and his son King Ahab, built royal palaces into its walls as well as an ivory house (that is, a house decorated with ivory) for Ahab's wife—the infamous Phoenician consort Queen Jezebel. This ivory house is referred to in 1 Kings 22:39, and excavations in the 1920s and 1930s uncovered fragments of ivory that are the remains of inlay originally placed on furniture that once adorned King Ahab's palace. Some of these ivory fragments are permanently housed in the Israel Museum, Jerusalem, and in other museums around the world, including the British Museum in London. The drawings on these ivories depict scenes of wild fauna and flora as well as mythological creatures (e.g. sphinxes and dragons) and foreign deities, and they show a Phoenician influence, as would be expected in view of the fact that Queen Jezebel was the daughter of the king of Phoenicia.

Another remarkable discovery that has been made by archaeologists during their excavations at Samaria is well worth mentioning. This is a feature found in the north-west corner of the royal compound and which is believed to be a pool, possibly the pool referred to in 1 Kings 22:38 where King Ahab's chariot was washed after he had been killed in battle and where prostitutes washed themselves. Whether these prostitutes were what we would today call 'sex workers' or whether they were temple prostitutes, or both, is open to debate.[1]

In 1 Kings 22:39 we read that King Ahab built cities during his reign, and although no specifics are given in the Bible the following archaeological discoveries fully support this biblical statement:

At Megiddo, Stratum IVA has been attributed to this king [Ahab]. There were a number of prominent structures associated with Stratum IVA, including an offset-inset fortification wall 12 ft wide, large pillared buildings, a palace, and a water system which included a 260 ft long tunnel. At Hazor, Stratum VIII is dated to the time of Ahab. As at Megiddo, the city was totally rebuilt at this time. A solid fortification wall 10 ft wide was constructed, along with a citadel, a large pillared building, and an underground water system. At Tel Dan, a well-preserved city gate was constructed in the days of Ahab in Stratum III. The high place, originally constructed by Jeroboam I (1 Kgs 12:28–30) and destroyed by Ben-Hadad king of Aram (1 Kgs 15:20), was reconstructed at this time.[2]

It can be seen, therefore, that modern archaeological discoveries give us confirmation of what is recorded in the Bible about King Ahab of the Northern Kingdom of Israel. This king did have a substantial mighty army; he did live in an ivory house—a palace that was full of furniture which was inlaid and decorated with ivory; and he was responsible for the building or rebuilding of many of the cities in his kingdom. After looking carefully at these and other archaeological discoveries pertaining to the life and times of King Ahab of the Northern Kingdom of Israel, Dr Bryant G. Wood has come to the following conclusion: 'All in all, archaeology has provided a great deal of evidence illuminating the reign of Ahab. It encompasses written, artifactual and architectural evidence, and fully substantiates the Biblical portrayal of this wicked, yet powerful, king.'[3]

Ahab and Jezebel—the demonic duo

In spite of all his architectural achievements, King Ahab of the Northern Kingdom of Israel is probably better known for his marriage to Jezebel, even though most people do not know much about her background. The Bible informs us that she was the daughter of Ethbaal, who was king of the maritime trade centre, Tyre, and its neighbouring port city, Sidon; these twin cities were the hub of Ethbaal's kingdom, Phoenicia. Ethbaal was also known as Ithobaal I; he was born in 915 BC and he died in 847 BC. He founded a new dynasty and during his reign Tyre expanded its territory as far north as Beirut and into the Mediterranean Sea to include a part of the island of Cyprus. Phoenicia was well known at the time for excess in personal and religious practices, and because of Phoenician's idolatry, the Bible frequently uses Tyre and Sidon as symbols of unholiness—see, for example, Isaiah 23; Ezekiel 26–28; Joel 3:4–8; Amos 1:9–10; and Zechariah 9:1–4. At the time that Jezebel married Ahab, Phoenicia comprised twenty-five cities, each retaining its separateness. Sidon was the oldest. Their marriage was probably one of convenience in order to cement relations between the Northern Kingdom of Israel and Phoenicia. Although it is not clear from the Bible, the marriage may have taken place when Ahab's father, Omri, was still king and while Ahab was a prince and the heir to his father's throne.

According to Geoffrey W. Bomiley, a prominent ecclesiastical and historical theologian and professor emeritus at Fuller Theological Seminary, having been professor of Church History and Historical Theology there from 1958 until his retirement in 1987, Jezebel, as a daughter of a Phoenician king who was a high priest of the god Baal, would probably have been a priestess of Phoenician deities, including Baal. This may explain why King Ahab early in his reign set up an altar to Baal in a temple of Baal in his capital Samaria so that Baal could be worshipped in the capital. It is obvious that although Jezebel may have changed her nationality when she got married, she did not change her religion. It is also obvious that although Jezebel's marriage to Ahab may have been an arranged marriage, the king was very much under her influence: he changed his religion and became a worshipper of Baal soon after marrying her. In doing so, he also started to change the religion of the people living in the Northern Kingdom of Israel, for they, too, started to worship Baal. As we shall see in the next section of this chapter, it took the great prophet Elijah on Mount Carmel to make them face up to the fact that they had to make the choice as to whether to follow the Lord or Baal.

When researching this book, I was amazed not to find any biblical references to Jezebel as a harlot or an adulteress. So often the name Jezebel is associated with a whore, an adulteress, a prostitute or a woman with a voracious sexual appetite. Yet I cannot find any scriptural reference to this. There are a couple of passages in the King James Version of the Bible that speak of the 'whoredoms' of Jezebel (2 Kings 9:22) and 'the whoredoms of the house of Ahab' (2 Chr. 21:13), but these are euphemisms for witchcraft and idolatry, as modern translations of the Scriptures illustrate by translating accordingly.

The reference to Jezebel in the letter to the church at Thyatira in Revelation 2:20–23 has nothing at all to do with King Ahab's wife but is a reference to a false prophetess in that church. Any reference to 'a painted Jezebel' is probably a reference to the story of Jezebel's death as recounted at the end of 2 Kings 9 and which we shall look at towards the end of this chapter: Queen Jezebel, knowing that she was about to be killed by King Jehu, put on eye make-up, arranged her hair and stood looking down at the street from a window in her palace in Jezreel, awaiting his arrival.

Elijah and the prophets of Baal on Mount Carmel

But let us go back to the beginning of King Ahab's reign. King Ahab's first test (or should we refer to it as Jezebel's first test?) of how strong Baal's power was came on Mount Carmel. No one can fail to be amazed at the Bible's introduction of the prophet Elijah onto the scene of time. Elijah went to King Ahab, who presumably was in his palace in Samaria, and told him that it would not rain for the next few years unless he, Elijah, said so! This sounds incredibly arrogant—until we realize who was speaking. It was one of the greatest prophets who ever lived. We also have to remember James's commentary on it: that this was the result of Elijah's fervent prayer (James 5:17). Other than that, we are informed that Elijah was an ordinary person just like us!

For the next three years, the Lord provided for Elijah in remarkable ways. First of all, the Lord told Elijah to go and live in a ravine and to drink water from the stream there; the Lord would provide food for him every morning and evening by means of ravens. This went on until the stream dried up. Then the Lord provided lodgings for Elijah with a widow in the village of Zarephath. During the time Elijah stayed there, the Lord miraculously provided food for the widow, her son and Elijah by ensuring that the flour, water and oil that the widow used to prepare her bread never ran out. During Elijah's stay with this widow, her son died, but through Elijah the Lord raised the widow's son from the dead.

The Lord then told Elijah to go and present himself to King Ahab and that he, the Lord, would then send rain upon the land. King Ahab had a faithful servant, Obadiah, who was a follower of the Lord and who had hidden and fed a hundred prophets of the Lord because Jezebel was seeking to kill them. King Ahab trusted Obadiah and commanded him to search the land for food for his livestock. On his travels, Obadiah met Elijah, and Elijah told him to go back and tell King Ahab that he, Elijah, would present himself to King Ahab that very day, which he did. When King Ahab met Elijah, he asked the prophet if he was the one who was troubling the Northern Kingdom of Israel; but Elijah replied that it was not he but King Ahab who was causing trouble, because he had abandoned the Lord and had followed Baal. Elijah then asked King Ahab to meet him on Mount Carmel with the 450 prophets of Baal and the 400 prophets of Asherah who ate at Jezebel's table. King Ahab agreed to this, and Elijah met with the people of the Northern Kingdom of Israel, the prophets of Baal and the prophets of Asherah on Mount Carmel.

On Mount Carmel Elijah challenged the people with the words 'How long will you waver[4] between two opinions?' (1 Kings 18:21, NIV), and then told them: 'If the LORD is God, follow him; but if Baal is God, follow him.' Interestingly, at first the people said nothing. Then Elijah suggested that they get two bulls and that the prophets of Baal should select one, cut it in pieces and put it on some wood, but put no fire under it; and he, Elijah, would do the same. Elijah then said that they should call on the name of their god; and the god who answered by fire would be declared to be God. All the people agreed.

Interestingly, Baal was considered to be a storm god, and one who would cause lightning (fire) to strike. Remember that it had not rained for three years, so the prophets of Baal were quite happy to believe that their god could produce a lightning strike and cause the bull sacrifice to be consumed with fire. Baal was a very important god to the people who lived in that area, where there was very little groundwater for irrigation, and rain and storms were vital. In this agricultural society, Baal and his consort, Asherah, were deemed essential for crops and fertility.

Elijah suggested that the prophets of Baal should go first. They danced around the altar that they had made and shouted to Baal to answer them, but fire did not fall from heaven and the sacrifice was not consumed. This went on until noon, when Elijah began to taunt them, suggesting that they should shout louder as perhaps Baal was (depending on which version of the Bible you read) day-dreaming, sleeping, busy, relieving himself or on a journey. These suggestions are in total contrast to what King David wrote about the Lord in Psalm 121, where he asserted that the Lord constantly watches over Israel and neither slumbers nor sleeps. At this, the prophets of Baal began to slash themselves with swords and spears, drawing blood from their wounds—but still Baal did not answer them.

This bloody ritual continued all afternoon until the time of the evening sacrifice. Elijah then told the people to come to him, and with twelve stones, each one representing one of the tribes of Israel, he repaired the altar of the Lord and dug a trench around the altar large enough to hold about 15 litres of water. He then arranged wood on the altar, cut the bull into pieces and laid it on the wood. Remember that it was a time of severe drought as it had not rained for three years. Elijah then asked the people to fill four large jars with water and to pour it over the offering and the wood. He asked them to do it again and then a third time. The Bible records that the water ran down the altar and even filled the trench—all 15 litres full!

Then Elijah prayed to the Lord, calling him the God of Abraham, Isaac and Israel, and simply asking the Lord to answer his prayer and to let the people know that he was God's servant and that the Lord was God in Israel and was turning the hearts of the people back to him. With that the fire of the Lord fell and consumed not only the sacrifice, but also the wood, the stones, the soil and the water that was in the trench. The Bible informs us that when the people saw this, they fell prostrate on the ground and cried out, 'The LORD—he is God!' (1 Kings 18:39, NIV). But Elijah had not finished. He told the people to seize the prophets of Baal (all 450 of them), and he had them brought down to the Kishon Valley, where he executed them.

King Ahab was present and saw all this taking place, but the Bible does not record his reaction. In fact, all we are told is that Elijah told King Ahab to go and eat and drink, for there was the sound of rain approaching. The king obeyed, but Elijah climbed to the top of Mount Carmel, prayed and sent his servant to look towards the sea for the approaching rain cloud. The seventh time the servant did so, he saw a cloud the size of a man's hand rising from the sea, and he notified Elijah, who immediately told his servant to tell King Ahab to hitch up his chariot and leave the area as soon as possible before the rain came and stopped him. The storm clouds came, the sky grew black and heavy rain began to pour. King Ahab did as Elijah's servant had commanded and rode off in his chariot from Mount Carmel to Jezreel, some 17 miles (27 km) away. The Bible, however, records that the power of the Lord came upon Elijah and he ran ahead of King Ahab's chariot all the way to Jezreel—what a sight that must have been!

It would be very easy to get carried away here with following the story of Elijah as it is recorded in the first book of Kings, but we will see more of his story in the next chapter.

King Ahab and his battles with King Benhadad of Syria

In 1 Kings 20 we read the remarkable story of how the Lord caused the defeat of the Syrian army led by King Benhadad. The story starts with the Syrian army supported by thirty-two other rulers with their horses and chariots besieging Samaria. King Benhadad was so confident of taking the city that he sent envoys into the city basically asking King Ahab to surrender all the silver and gold and the best of his wives and the children. King Ahab agreed to these terms of surrender and the envoys returned to King Benhadad and informed him. The envoys then returned to King Ahab and told him that the next day King Benhadad would send his officials to search King Ahab's palace and houses and seize anything of value and carry it away. On hearing this, King Ahab summoned his officials, who advised him to inform King Benhadad that this demand could not be met. The envoys left and informed King Benhadad of King Ahab's decision.

King Benhadad responded with the cheeky boast that his soldiers would destroy Samaria and carry the rubble away in their hands, to which King Ahab responded that a real soldier did his boasting after the battle, not before it. Interestingly, the king of Syria made his boast and heard King Ahab's response to it while he and the other kings were drinking in their tents. Meanwhile, a prophet told King Ahab not to be afraid of the huge Syrian army because the Lord would give him victory over the Syrians that very day.

King Ahab began the attack on the Syrian army at noon, at the time when King Benhadad and his thirty-two allies were getting drunk in their tents. The young soldiers from King Ahab's army advanced first and scouts from King Benhadad's army reported to him that a group of soldiers was coming out of Samaria. King Benhadad ordered that the soldiers be killed, whether they were coming to fight or to ask for peace. The young soldiers fought hard, as did King Ahab's army, and as a result the army of the Northern Kingdom of Israel inflicted a heavy defeat on the Syrian army. But God had not yet finished. Through the prophet, he told King Ahab to build up his forces and make careful plans because the king of Syria would attack again the following spring. And this is what happened.

The Syrians thought that King Ahab's army had defeated them because they had 'mountain gods,' so they believed that they could defeat King Ahab if they fought his army on the plains the following spring. King Benhadad's officials advised him to replace all the kings that were in his army with new officers and also to replace all the horses and chariots with new horses and chariots, so he basically had a new army with which he could fight King Ahab's army on the plains. Through a prophet, the Lord again promised victory to King Ahab, even though his army was far outnumbered by the Syrian army. For seven days the two armies camped and faced each other, and then they began to fight. The Bible records that King Ahab's army killed one hundred thousand Syrian soldiers, and the rest of the Syrian army escaped into the city of Aphek, where the city walls fell on twenty-seven thousand of them. Again we see that the Lord gave another victory to King Ahab against seemingly insurmountable odds.

King Benhadad also escaped into the city of Aphek and managed to hide with some of his officials in the back room of a house. The officials told the king that they had heard that King Ahab was a merciful king, and suggested to Benhadad that they should approach King Ahab with sackcloth around their waists and ropes around their necks and plead for the life of King Benhadad. When they did this, King Ahab asked them to bring King Benhadad to join him in his chariot, where they made a treaty with each other and King Ahab set King Benhadad free. This displeased the Lord, and a prophet of the Lord told King Ahab that because he had let King Benhadad go free, King Ahab's life would be taken and the Northern Kingdom of Israel would be given to another. We shall see in a later section how King Ahab met his death, and we shall see in the next chapter how King Jehu became king of the Northern King of Israel.

King Ahab and Naboth's vineyard

As we have seen, King Ahab and his wife Queen Jezebel had a palace in the city of Jezreel which lay about 21 miles (34 km) north of the capital city of Samaria. Near to this palace was a vineyard owned by Naboth, who is referred to as a Jezreelite, meaning that he and his forefathers had lived in Jezreel for perhaps about 550 years, since the time the Israelites had invaded the land of Canaan.[5] King Ahab wanted to own Naboth's vineyard and use it for a vegetable garden, so he offered to purchase it from Naboth, and in fact offered to give him a better vineyard in exchange if Naboth preferred. King Ahab offered Naboth whatever it was worth.

Now, to understand the story about King Ahab and Naboth's vineyard and all its implications, we really need to understand a small but important piece of the Law given by the Lord to Moses which is recorded in Leviticus 25:23: 'The land must not be sold permanently, because the land is mine and you are but aliens and my tenants' (NIV 1984). Naboth knew that, according to God's Law, he could not sell the land—not even to the king—and so he refused. This upset King Ahab, who went to his palace and sulked.

When Jezebel saw her husband sulking, she asked him what was wrong, so he told her. Now, instead of realizing that 'no man is above the law' (a phrase attributed to Theodore Roosevelt, the 26th President of the United States of America, and one that certainly should be applied to King Ahab), Queen Jezebel said that she would get the vineyard for her husband, and she hatched a devious plan in order to obtain the vineyard for him.

Jezebel wrote a letter in King Ahab's name and even sealed it with his seal. She sent it to the elders and nobles who lived in the same city as Naboth, telling them to proclaim a day of fasting. She asked them to seat two scoundrels opposite Naboth and to have them testify that Naboth had cursed both God and the king, upon which they were to take him out and stone him to death. They did this, and reported back to Jezebel when the evil deed was done. As soon as Jezebel heard the news that Naboth was dead, she told her husband King Ahab the news, and he went and took possession of Naboth's vineyard.

The deaths of Ahab and Jezebel

But nothing is hidden from God's sight, and the Lord revealed to Elijah what King Ahab had done. God told Elijah to go to meet King Ahab in Naboth's vineyard and say to him that in the place where dogs had licked up Naboth's blood, dogs would lick up his blood. Through Elijah the Lord also told King Ahab that his dynasty would not be established—we shall see in the next chapter how the Lord used King Jehu to accomplish this. Also through Elijah the Lord told King Ahab that dogs would devour the body of his wife, Jezebel, by the wall of Jezreel, and that any of his relatives who died in the city would be eaten by dogs and any who died in the countryside would be eaten by vultures. When King Ahab heard this, he tore his clothes, put on sackcloth and fasted, and, to quote the Scriptures, 'went about gloomy and depressed' (1 Kings 21:27, GNT). When the Lord saw this, he told Elijah that he would cause all this to happen, not in King Ahab's day, but during his son's lifetime.

At this time the Northern Kingdom of Israel and the Southern Kingdom of Judah lived peaceably with one another and their kings, Ahab and Jehoshaphat, respectively, got on reasonably well. The Bible records in 1 Kings 22:1 that for three years there had been peace between Syria and the Northern Kingdom of Israel, but King Ahab was not happy because the Syrians still had control of the city of Ramoth Gilead, which was in the Northern Kingdom of Israel. King Ahab asked King Jehoshaphat of the Southern Kingdom of Judah if he would go with him to attack the city to reclaim it. King Jehoshaphat said he was happy to do so, but suggested that they first consulted the Lord, which they did.

Only one prophet, Micaiah, spoke the word of the Lord truthfully, and this was to tell the kings that if they attacked the city of Ramoth Gilead, King Ahab would be killed in the battle. But the kings took no notice of Micaiah and went into battle, and, at King Ahab's suggestion, King Jehoshaphat dressed in his royal robes and King Ahab went in disguise—presumably to prevent his being recognized as the king of the Northern Kingdom of Israel and therefore being killed in the battle. They hoped that the Syrians would attack King Jehoshaphat, not King Ahab. At first their plan worked. The king of Syria ordered his charioteers—all thirty-two of them—to attack the king of Israel, and when they first saw

King Jehoshaphat, they thought he was King Ahab. But when they heard him shouting, they realized he was not King Ahab, so they stopped attacking him. Then, by chance—if there is such a thing when we are dealing with the Lord and his will—one of the Syrian soldiers shot an arrow, and this struck King Ahab between the joints of his armour and fatally wounded him. King Ahab ordered the driver of his chariot to turn around and pull out of the battle. The blood from his wound ran down and covered the floor of his chariot and King Ahab died in the evening. King Ahab's body was taken back to the city of Samaria, where he was buried, and his chariot was cleaned at the pool of Samaria, where dogs licked up his blood as the Lord, through the prophet Elijah, had said would happen.

The death of Queen Jezebel is recorded at the end at the end of 2 Kings 9. We mentioned this briefly earlier in this chapter when we were considering the phrase 'painted Jezebel'. Queen Jezebel, knowing that she was about to be killed by the newly crowned King Jehu of the Northern Kingdom of Israel, put on eye make-up, arranged her hair and stood looking down at the street from a window in her palace in Jezreel, awaiting his arrival. When King Jehu came through the gate, she sarcastically called him 'Zimri', the name of the unscrupulous predecessor of her father-in-law, King Omri. Zimri had ruled the Northern Kingdom of Israel for a mere seven days after he had murdered King Elah and usurped the throne. King Jehu was furious and ordered the eunuchs who were with Jezebel to throw her out of the window, which they did. Some of her blood spattered onto the wall and the horses, and King Jehu drove his horses and chariot over her body and then entered the palace.

Only after he had eaten a meal did King Jehu command his men to take care of the body of Jezebel, whom he called 'that cursed woman', and bury her, for she was a king's daughter. However, when they went to bury her, all they found was her skull and her hands and feet. When King Jehu was informed of this, he declared that this was the fulfilment of

Elijah's prophecy mentioned above and recorded in 1 Kings 21:23: that the dogs would devour the flesh of Jezebel in Jezreel and that no one would be able to say of her remains, 'This is Jezebel.'

Summary and conclusion

We have seen that during the reign of King Omri, he arranged the marriage of his son Ahab to the Phoenician princess Jezebel, who was the daughter of Ethbaal, the king of Sidon. Following his marriage, King Ahab introduced Baal worship widely into the Northern Kingdom of Israel. After three years of drought, the great prophet Elijah challenged the people to decide which god they would follow—the Lord or Baal. The Lord answered by fire and the people decided to follow the Lord.

In addition to his capital in Samaria, King Ahab maintained a palace at Jezreel, some 21 miles (34 km) to the north. Adjacent to this palace was a fine vineyard owned by Naboth, which King Ahab desired. Through Jezebel's scheming, Naboth was murdered and King Ahab acquired the vineyard. Because of this, King Ahab's entire family was condemned to death by the prophet Elijah. King Ahab died in battle against the Syrians at Ramoth Gilead, after which his body was taken to Samaria, where it was buried.

The Bible portrays King Ahab of the Northern Kingdom of Israel as a prosperous and powerful king and a great architect and builder. Archaeology fully substantiates this portrayal of this wicked yet powerful king. King Ahab's downfall was that he married a woman who did not believe in following the Lord, but who was a follower of Baal. Her manoeuvrings to get Naboth's vineyard for her husband showed her complete disregard of and disdain for the Law of the Lord. This was the last straw for the Lord and it resulted in the Lord's judgement for both Ahab and his wife. Today, archaeologists think they may have discovered the pool referred to in Scripture where Ahab's chariot was washed after he was killed. This is where, in fulfilment of Elijah's prophecy, dogs licked up King Ahab's blood—a sad end for a king!

NOTES

1 See the commentaries on 1 Kings 22:38 at Bible Hub, https://biblehub.com/commentaries/1_kings/22-38.htm.

2 Bryant G. Wood, 'Ahab the Israelite', *Bible and Spade* (Fall 1996); reproduced at 'The Shiloh Excavations', Associates for Biblical Research, https://biblearchaeology.org/research/divided-kingdom/3584-ahab-the-israelite.

3 Ibid.

4 In the original Hebrew, the word used conveys limping or hobbling, hence in the King James Version the word used is 'halt', conveying that the people were actually crippled and so were unable to make up their minds in which direction to go.

5 This is assuming that the exodus took place in about 1446 BC and that the Israelites conquered the land of Canaan forty years later.

King Jehu of the Northern Kingdom of Israel

After the prophet Elijah had killed all the prophets of Baal in the Kishon Valley and King Ahab had returned to Jezreel and told his wife Jezebel all that had happened on Mount Carmel, Jezebel threatened to kill Elijah, and so Elijah fled for his life with his servant and went to Beer Sheba in the Southern Kingdom of Judah. Eventually, sustained by food miraculously supplied by an angel, Elijah made his way to Mount Sinai and into a cave to spend the night. In this cave the Lord spoke to Elijah in 'a still small voice', as the King James Version of the Bible puts it in 1 Kings 19:12. The Lord asked Elijah what he was doing there, and Elijah replied that he was the only one who was left to serve the Lord and that everyone was trying to kill him. The Lord then informed Elijah that he was not the only one who served the Lord—there were seven thousand who were loyal to the Lord and who had not bowed the knee to Baal. The Lord also instructed Elijah to do three things. He was to anoint Hazael as king of Syria; he was to anoint Jehu son[1] of Nimshi as king of the Northern Kingdom of Israel; and he was to anoint Elisha the son of Shaphat from Abel Meholah to succeed him as a prophet. These events all took place, but not immediately or in that order.

Although Elijah was commanded by the Lord to anoint Jehu as king, Jehu was actually anointed by another prophet (we do not know his name because the Bible does not record it) on the instructions of Elisha, who succeeded Elijah. At the time, the army of the Northern Kingdom of Israel was at war with the Syrians at Ramoth Gilead. Elisha instructed one of the young prophets to go to Ramoth Gilead and take a jar of olive oil with him; when he got there, he was to search for Jehu, who was a commander in the army. The prophet was to take him into a private room away from his companions and pour the olive oil on his head, telling him that the Lord proclaimed him king of the Northern Kingdom of Israel.

The prophet did as instructed by Elisha, took Jehu into a private room, anointed him, and gave him what can only be described as his commission from the Lord:

You are to kill your master the king, that son of Ahab, so that I may punish Jezebel for murdering my prophets and my other servants. All Ahab's family and descendants are to die; I will get rid of every male in his family . . . as I did the families of King Jeroboam of Israel and of King Baasha of Israel. (2 Kings 9:7–9, GNT)

The young prophet then left the room and fled. Jehu returned to his fellow officers, who asked what the prophet (he is actually called a 'madman' in the NIV 1984 and a 'crazy fellow' in the GNT) had wanted with him. When Jehu told them, his fellow officers spread their cloaks on the top of the steps for Jehu to stand on, blew their trumpets and shouted, 'Jehu is king!' Whether they did this in jest or not is not clear. But one thing is clear. Immediately, Jehu took on the role of king of the Northern Kingdom of Israel and began to carry out the commission that the Lord, through the unnamed prophet, had given him.

Although, like King Omri, Jehu was a commander in the army, unlike King Omri it appears that King Jehu was an Israelite and not a foreigner. We are told that his father was Jehoshaphat—not to be confused with King Jehoshaphat of the Southern Kingdom of Judah—and that his grandfather was Nimshi. He may also have been a great-grandson of King Omri.[2]

King Jehu fulfils his commission

Throughout this section it will be advisable to keep referring to the family tree shown in Figure 3 on page 89 in order to understand which monarch is meant. When King Ahab of the Northern Kingdom of Israel died in 853 BC, his son Ahaziah succeeded him as king, and the Bible records that he followed the wicked example of his parents (King Ahab and Queen Jezebel) and that he worshipped and served Baal. He reigned for only two years (one actual year), and the first chapter of the second book of Kings is taken up with describing how he was seriously injured when he fell from the balcony of the roof of his palace in his capital Samaria, and how he sent some messengers to consult Baalzebub, the god of the Philistine city of Ekron, to find out if he would recover from his injuries.

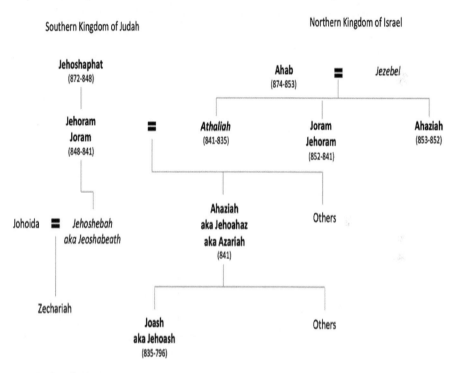

Figure 3: Family tree of the kings of the Northern Kingdom of Israel and the Southern Kingdom of Judah

However, the angel of the Lord had commanded the prophet Elijah to go and meet the messengers of King Ahaziah on their way to Ekron and ask them why they were going to consult Baalzebub the god of Ekron. Was it because they thought there was no god in Israel? Elijah then told the messengers that they were to return to King Ahaziah and tell him that the Lord said he would not recover from his injuries but that he would die because, by seeking counsel from the heathen god of the Philistines, he was acting as though there was no God in Israel. When the messengers returned to the king in Samaria, he asked them why they had returned; when they told him, King Ahaziah asked what the man they had met looked like. When they described him as wearing a cloak made of camel's hair tied with a leather thong, the king recognized him as Elijah, for Elijah had had dealings with King Ahaziah's father, King Ahab, on many occasions, and King Ahaziah would have recognized him from this description.

King Ahaziah of the Northern Kingdom of Israel had no sons, so his brother Joram became king of the Northern Kingdom of Israel. King Joram was the king under whom Jehu was serving when the unnamed prophet had anointed him king, and he was the king whom the Lord instructed Jehu to kill. At the time, King Joram was at Jezreel recovering from wounds that he had received in the battle at Ramoth Gilead when the army of the Northern Kingdom of Israel was fighting the army of King Hazael of Syria. Determined to obey the Lord's instructions, Jehu informed his fellow officers that they were not to let anyone go out of Ramoth Gilead and warn the people in Jezreel of what was happening. Jehu then got into his chariot and drove from Ramoth Gilead to Jezreel, a distance of about 45 miles (just over 70 km), to visit King Joram.

King Ahaziah of the Southern Kingdom of Judah was also in Jezreel at this time, visiting King Joram of the Northern Kingdom of Israel. If you look carefully back at the family tree in Figure 3 on page 89, you will see that King Ahaziah of the Southern Kingdom of Judah was the son of King

Jehoram (also known as King Joram) of the Southern Kingdom of Judah, who in turn was the son of King Jehoshaphat of the Southern Kingdom of Judah. King Ahaziah of the Southern Kingdom of Judah was therefore the grandson of King Jehoshaphat of the Southern Kingdom of Judah. King Ahaziah was also the grandson (via Queen Athaliah of the Southern Kingdom of Judah) of King Ahab of the Northern Kingdom of Israel. All these different relationships were the result of intermarriages between the royal houses of the Northern Kingdom of Israel and the Southern Kingdom of Judah at this time.

As King Jehu and his men approached the city of Jezreel, the watchman saw them and informed King Joram of the Northern Kingdom of Israel, who gave instructions to approach them to find out if they were friends or foes. The messengers rode out, and when they asked King Jehu if he and his men were friends or enemies, he told them that it was none of their business, and instructed them to fall in and ride behind him, which they did. This happened again. The third time it happened, the watchman reported that the leader of the group was driving his chariot like a madman, just like Jehu. It would appear that Jehu had a reputation for driving his chariot 'furiously', as the King James Version of the Bible puts it in 2 Kings 9:20. King Joram then asked for his chariot to be made ready, and he and King Ahaziah of the Southern Kingdom of Judah rode out to meet King Jehu. Ironically, they met King Jehu in the field that had once belonged to Naboth. King Joram, whose parents (King Ahab and his wife Jezebel) had been instrumental in the death of Naboth, asked King Jehu if he was coming in peace. King Jehu asked how there could be peace when all the witchcraft and idolatry that King Joram's mother, Jezebel, had started still existed. King Joram replied that this was treason, turned his chariot around and began to hurry away. King Jehu then drew his bow and with all his strength shot an arrow that struck King Joram in the back but pierced his heart, with the result that he fell and died in his chariot. King Jehu asked his aide to remove King Joram's body from the chariot and throw it into the field that had belonged to Naboth.

When King Ahaziah of the Southern Kingdom of Judah saw what had happened, he fled in his chariot towards the town of Beth Haggan, pursued by King Jehu and his men. King Jehu was determined to kill him too, in accordance with the instructions given to him by the unnamed prophet when he was anointed king. Remember that King Ahaziah of the Southern Kingdom of Judah was the grandson of King Ahab, so by killing him, King Jehu would be killing a descendant of King Ahab. King Jehu's men eventually caught up with King Ahaziah and wounded him as he drove his chariot, and here the Bible gives a precise location: 'on the road up to Gur, near the town of Ibleam' (GNT). King Ahaziah managed to keep going until he reached the city of Megiddo, where he died. His officials took Ahaziah's body back to Jerusalem, where he was buried in the royal tombs in David's City. King Ahaziah's death occurred in the year 841 BC.

The next relative of King Ahab whom King Jehu killed was King Ahab's widow, Jezebel. We saw at the end of the last chapter exactly how he carried this out.

King Jehu could only be described as fervent in his duty to obey the command of the Lord given him through the unnamed prophet. We read in 2 Kings 10:1 that there were seventy descendants of King Ahab living in the capital city of Samaria. The New International Version says that these descendants were his 'sons', but this is not at all clear—some of them may have been his grandchildren. King Jehu wrote a letter to the guardians of these descendants with copies to the officials and to the elders of the cities of Samaria and Jezreel. In this letter he asked the guardians to appoint the best and most worthy of their master's sons and to set him on his father's throne and then fight for their master's house. When they read this they were terrified, reasoning that if King Joram and King Ahaziah could not defeat King Jehu, how could they?

As a result, they, together with the palace administrator, the city governor and the city elders, sent a message to King Jehu saying that they would not appoint anyone as king, and asking King Jehu to do whatever he thought best.

King Jehu then wrote them a second letter, in which he requested that they take the heads of their master's sons and meet him at the city of Jezreel the following day. Those who were bringing up the seventy royal princes executed them, put their heads in baskets and sent them to Jezreel, where King Jehu placed them in two piles at the entrance of the city gate until the following morning. King Jehu then addressed the people who had gathered there, explaining that he was responsible for killing King Joram and that the heads of the royal princes at the entrance of the city gate were proof that the Lord had done what he said he would do through the prophet Elijah. King Jehu then put to death all the other relatives of King Ahab who were living in Jezreel and all his officers, close friends and priests.

King Jehu then left Jezreel to go to Samaria. On the way there, at a place called 'Shepherds' Camp', he met some relatives of the late King Ahaziah of the Southern Kingdom of Judah. King Jehu asked them who they were and they answered that they were King Ahaziah's relatives and that they were going to Jezreel to visit the families of Queen Jezebel and the rest of the royal family. King Jehu ordered his men to take them alive, which they did, before slaughtering all forty-two of them. King Jehu continued his journey to Samaria, where he killed all of King Ahab's relatives who were living there, not sparing even one. King Jehu was meticulous in carrying out the Lord's commission to him via the unnamed prophet that 'all Ahab's family and descendants are to die'—die at King Jehu's hands they did!

Eradicating Baal worship from the land

When King Jehu arrived at the capital city of Samaria, not only did he kill all of King Ahab's relatives, but he also killed those who worshipped Baal. He did this by feigning that he worshipped Baal more fervently than King Ahab had done. He called all the people of Samaria together and told them to tell all the prophets, priests and worshippers of Baal that he was going to offer a great sacrifice to Baal. He said that no one was to be excused; anyone who was not present would be put to death. However, this was a ploy on his part in order to kill all the followers of Baal and to eradicate the worship of Baal from the Northern Kingdom of Israel. A day of worship in honour of Baal was proclaimed throughout the land, and all those who worshipped Baal came to the temple of Baal in Samaria—this was the temple King Ahab had built when he married Jezebel. The Bible informs us that the temple was filled from one end to the other with Baal worshippers.

King Jehu continued with his deception with the help of Jonadab, whom he had met when he was on his way from Jezreel to Samaria and who had informed King Jehu that he was totally committed to the Lord and therefore to King Jehu. King Jehu ordered the keeper of the sacred robes to bring out the robes for the ministers of Baal, and then King Jehu, accompanied by Jonadab, went into the temple of Baal and instructed the people to make sure that there were no worshippers of the Lord present. It cannot be overemphasized that King Jehu was *not* a Baal worshipper, and any act of sacrifice and burnt offering to Baal that he performed was an act of deception to lull the Baal worshippers in the temple into a false sense of security. As soon as King Jehu had finished his acts of sacrifice and offerings to Baal in the temple, he instructed the eighty guards that he had posted outside the temple to enter the temple and to kill all those who were in the temple and who were Baal worshippers, and to make sure that none escaped. The bodies of the slaughtered Baal worshippers were then brought out of the temple, the temple was demolished, and thereafter it was used as a public lavatory!

Although King Jehu of the Northern Kingdom of Israel eradicated

Baal worship in the land, for some reason he did not destroy the golden calves that King Jeroboam I had placed in Dan and Bethel. Remember that these were the idols that King Jeroboam I had placed in these cities when he informed the people living in the Northern Kingdom of Israel of the fake news that these were the gods that had brought them out of Egypt. A thousand years after the exodus and some ninety years after the reign of Jeroboam I, some of the people in the Northern Kingdom of Israel still believed the lie that the golden calves in Dan and Bethel were the gods that had delivered them out of Egypt. This begs the question whether King Jehu also believed this, and whether this was why he did not destroy these idols. The Bible explains that because King Jehu did not turn away from the sins of King Jeroboam I, the Lord began to reduce the size of the Northern Kingdom of Israel, as the kingdom of Syria expanded into its territory. Little else about King Jehu is recorded for us in the Scriptures other than that he reigned for twenty-eight official years (twenty-seven actual years), from 841 to 814 BC, and that he was buried in Samaria.

King Jehu's dynasty

Before King Jehu died, however, the Lord spoke to him and commended him for killing all of King Ahab's descendants, and in return promised him that his descendants to the fourth generation would rule over the Northern Kingdom of Israel. We will look briefly at each of King Jehu's descendants in turn and see what they actually achieved as they ruled over the Northern Kingdom of Israel.

When King Jehu died in 814 BC his son Jehoahaz became king, and he reigned for seventeen official years (sixteen actual years), from 814 to 798 BC. We read about his reign in 2 Kings 13:1–9, where we learn that King Jehoahaz led the people in the evil ways of King Jeroboam I and that the Northern Kingdom of Israel was defeated again and again by the Syrians. When King Jehoahaz prayed to the Lord, he sent him a leader, who is not named, who freed the Northern Kingdom of Israel from the Syrians, and as a result the people in the Northern Kingdom of Israel lived in peace, although they kept on sinning and worshipping the goddess Asherah.

King Jehoahaz died in 798 BC and was succeeded by his son Jehoash, who reigned for sixteen years, from 798 to 782 BC. Although it is not mentioned in the Scriptures, a stela found in 1967 at Tell al Rimah, about 50 miles (about 80 km) west of Mosul in Iraq, refers to this king paying tribute to the Assyrian King Adad-nirari III. This is further proof that the kings who are mentioned in the Bible were real historical individuals and not the mythical monarchs they were once thought to be. Before such archaeological finds were uncovered in the nineteenth and twentieth centuries, many so-called scholars ridiculed the Scriptures, believing that the stories of Israel and its kings recorded in the Old Testament were no more than myths and legends. Such so-called scholars had to change their minds rapidly as one archaeological find after another proved that what was written in the historical books of the Bible was straightforward history. It cannot be overemphasized that the history written in the Old Testament is not a work of fiction but reliable history that can be trusted.

The life of King Jehoash is closely linked with the life of King Amaziah, who was the son of King Joash of the Southern Kingdom of Judah, whom we will be looking at in detail in the next chapter. When King Joash of the Southern Kingdom of Judah died in 796 BC, his son Amaziah succeeded him as king and led a campaign to gain control over Edom, which had been lost by King Jehoram, the son of King Jehoshaphat of the Southern Kingdom of Judah. Being in control of Edom was important, for it meant controlling the southern trade routes in and out of the Southern Kingdom of Judah. King Amaziah hired a large contingent of soldiers from the Northern Kingdom of Israel (a hundred thousand, according to 2 Chr. 25:6) to help him with his campaign. However, after advice from 'a man of God', he dismissed these soldiers from the Northern Kingdom of Israel. These troops took this as an insult and vented their feelings by attacking and plundering various towns in the Southern Kingdom of Judah on their way back to their homes in the Northern Kingdom of Israel.

When King Amaziah of the Southern Kingdom of Judah returned triumphant from Edom to his own land, he brought back with him some of the gods of the people of Edom. Unbelievably, King Amaziah set up these idols as his own gods and bowed down to them and burned sacrifices to them. Needless to say, the Lord was very angry with King Amaziah and sent a prophet to speak to him about this, but the king refused to listen to the prophet and interrupted what he had to say, warning the prophet that if he did not stop talking, he would have him killed. The prophet stopped talking, but not before telling King Amaziah that God had decided to destroy him because he had ignored the Lord's advice. King Amaziah of the Southern Kingdom of Judah then plotted against the Northern Kingdom of Israel and sent a message to King Jehoash of the Northern Kingdom of Israel, challenging him to a fight. King Jehoash responded by suggesting that King Amaziah should give his daughter to King Jehoash's son in marriage, and advised King Amaziah to stay at home.

King Amaziah, however, refused to listen and went to war against King Jehoash, but King Amaziah's army was defeated. King Jehoash took King Amaziah prisoner and took him to Jerusalem, where King Jehoash's army tore down about 600 feet (about 180 metres) of the city walls. They looted the gold and silver and the palace articles that were in the temple and took them, together with King Amaziah and hostages, back to their own capital city of Samaria in the Northern Kingdom of Israel.

One of the problems we have in following the story of what happened in the Southern Kingdom of Judah after King Amaziah was taken captive to Samaria is that the accounts written in 2 Kings 14:17–22 and 2 Chronicles 25:23–28 and 26:1–3 are *not* written chronologically. This has been ably demonstrated by Professor Thiele, who managed to work out the correct chronological sequence for what happened at this time.[3]

As soon as King Amaziah was taken captive to Samaria by King Jehoash, the people in the Southern Kingdom of Judah appointed King Amaziah's son, Uzziah, who was also called Azariah, as their king. The problem is that, from reading the Bible, you get the impression that this event happened *after* King Amaziah had been released from prison in Samaria, but actually it happened *before*. King Amaziah remained in prison in Samaria until the death of King Jehoash of the Northern Kingdom of Israel in 782 BC. He was then released and returned to the Southern Kingdom of Judah, where he lived for the next fifteen years. Because of opposition to his being king (remember his son, Uzziah, who was also called Azariah, was reigning as king at the time), he did not occupy his throne in Jerusalem, but fled to the town of Lachish, some 30 miles (about 48 km) south-west of Jerusalem. King Amaziah was eventually assassinated there in 767 BC and his body was returned on horseback to Jerusalem, where he was buried in the royal tombs of David's City.

When King Jehoash of the Northern Kingdom of Israel died in 782 BC, he was succeeded by his son Jeroboam II, who had already been reigning as co-regent with King Jehoash for twelve actual years.[4] He then reigned solely until he died in 753 BC. The Bible informs us that Jeroboam II was a very evil king. However, he had one redeeming feature: he was very strong militarily, for the Bible tells us that he took part in brave battles and that he recovered for the Northern Kingdom of Israel both Damascus and Hamath, and other holdings taken by King Hazael of Syria. When King Jeroboam II died, his son Zechariah succeeded him as king of the Northern Kingdom of Israel. However, like his father, he was also an evil king, and after he had reigned for only six months he was assassinated by Shallum, son of Jabesh, at Ibleam, a Levitical city west of the Jordan River between Samaria and Jezreel. King Zechariah was the fourth generation from King Jehu. Hence the Lord had kept the promise he had made to King Jehu: that his descendants down to the fourth generation would be kings of the Northern Kingdom of Israel.

Before leaving this section, it is worth pointing out that the prophet Jonah ministered at the time when Jeroboam II reigned over the Northern Kingdom of Israel. We know this from the reference to the prophet Jonah in 2 Kings 14:25. We know that Jeroboam II reigned from 793 to 753 BC. Very often people want to know which king of Assyria, and therefore which king of Nineveh, was ruling at that time. The names of the kings of Assyria at the time of Jeroboam II and the dates when they reigned are as follows:

- Adad-nirari III   811–783 BC
- Shalmaneser IV   783–773 BC
- Ashur-dan III   773–755 BC
- Ashur-nirari V   755–745 BC

As the Bible does not name the king of Assyria and consequently the name of the king of Nineveh when Jonah preached his message of repentance to the citizens of that great city, and as no records from Assyria or Nineveh have yet been found naming that king, we are unable at this time to identify him.

King Jehu in archaeology

King Jehu is mentioned on the Black Obelisk of Shalmaneser III, which is

a black limestone Assyrian sculpture with many scenes in bas-relief and inscriptions. It comes from Nimrud (ancient Kalhu), in northern Iraq, and commemorates the deeds of King Shalmaneser III (reigned from 858–824 BC). It is on display at the British Museum in London, and several other museums have cast replicas.

It is the most complete Assyrian obelisk yet discovered, and is historically significant because it is thought to display the earliest ancient depiction of a biblical figure—Jehu, King of Israel . . . Its reference to *Parsua* is also the first known reference to the Persians.

Tribute offerings are shown being brought from identifiable regions and peoples. It was erected as a public monument in 825 BC at a time of civil war, in the central square of Nimrud ... It was discovered by archaeologist Sir Austen Henry Layard in 1846 ...

It features twenty relief scenes, five on each side. They depict five different subdued kings, bringing tribute and prostrating [themselves] before the Assyrian king. From top to bottom they are: (1) Sua of Gilzanu (in north-west Iran), (2) 'Jehoram of Bit Omri' ([Jehu] of the House of Omri), (3) an unnamed ruler of Musri (probably Egypt), (4) Marduk-apil-usur of Suhi (middle Euphrates, Syria and Iraq), and (5) Qalparunda of Patin (Antakya region of Turkey). Each scene occupies four panels around the monument and is described by a cuneiform script above them.

On the top and the bottom of the reliefs there is a long cuneiform inscription recording the annals of Shalmaneser III. It lists the military campaigns which the king and his commander-in-chief headed every year, until the thirty-first year of his reign. Some features might suggest that the work had been commissioned by the commander-in-chief, Dayyan-Assur.[5]

On the Black Obelisk we actually see a portrait of Jehu, or of Jehu's ambassador, bowing before King Shalmaneser III, and above the scene is written in Assyrian cuneiform: 'The tribute of Jehu, son of Omri: I received from him silver, gold, a golden bowl, a golden vase with pointed bottom, golden tumblers, golden buckets, tin, a staff for a king [and] spears.'[6]

The Assyrian name used for Jehu was *Yaw* and, as noted in Chapter 3, it was customary on Assyrian royal inscriptions to refer to a royal dynasty by its founder (*Omri*), even though King Jehu of the Northern Kingdom of Israel was, in fact, unrelated to King Omri and, as we have seen in this chapter, had enthusiastically killed all of King Omri's descendants by killing all of his son's (that is, King Ahab's) descendants.

Summary and conclusion

Jehu was a commander in the army of King Joram of the Northern

Kingdom of Israel who was chosen by the Lord to be king. When he was anointed, he was commanded to kill not only his master, King Joram, but all of King Ahab's family and descendants. As we have seen, King Jehu carried this out meticulously and fervently; no one can say that King Jehu did not carry out the commission that the Lord had given him.

By subterfuge King Jehu eradicated Baal worship from the Northern Kingdom of Israel. However, for some reason he did not destroy the golden calves that King Jeroboam I had placed in Dan and Bethel. Before King Jehu died, the Lord commended him for killing all of King Ahab's descendants, and promised him that his descendants to the fourth generation would rule over the Northern Kingdom of Israel—which is what happened.

We know that King Jehu was a real historical king for he is mentioned not only in the Bible, but also on the Black Obelisk of Shalmaneser III. Although there are no other archaeological finds relating directly to King Jehu of the Northern Kingdom of Israel, a stela found in 1967 refers to King Jehoash, King Jehu's grandson, paying tribute to the Assyrian King Adad-nirari III. This is further proof that the kings mentioned in the Bible were real people, and that we can trust what is written in the historical books of the Old Testament—including the fact that King Jehu drove his chariot '*furiously*', as the King James Version describes it in 2 Kings 9:20.

NOTES

1 Jehu was actually the grandson of Nimshi.

2 'Jehu', Wikipedia, citing Amitai Baruchi-Unna, 'Jehuites, Ahabites, and Omrides Blood Kinship and Bloodshed', Journal for the Study of the Old Testament, 41.1 (2017), pp. 3–21.

3 Edwin R. Thiele, The Mysterious Numbers of the Hebrew Kings, new rev. edn (Grand Rapids, MI: Kregel, 1994), pp. 113–116.

4 Ibid., pp. 111–118.

5 'Black Obelisk of Shalmaneser III', Wikipedia, https://en.wikipedia.org/wiki/Black_Obelisk_of_Shalmaneser_III.

6 Ibid.

Chapter 5

King Joash of the Southern Kingdom of Judah

I n this chapter we shall be looking at the life of King Joash of the Southern Kingdom of Judah, but to understand his life and the times in which he lived, we need to fully understand his family background. We have already looked in detail at the life of King Ahab and his father, King Omri, who were kings of the Northern Kingdom of Israel. Joash, king of the Southern Kingdom of Judah, was King Ahab's great-grandson. His descent from his great-grandfathers King Ahab of the Northern Kingdom of Israel and King Jehoshaphat of the Southern Kingdom of Judah is shown in the family tree in Figure 3 on page 89. Throughout this chapter it will be advisable to keep referring to this family tree. King Jehoshaphat was the great-great-great-grandson of King David, and the family tree shows how, for a time, descendants of the royal house of the Southern Kingdom of Judah married descendants of the royal house of the Northern Kingdom of Israel. Furthermore, the family tree reveals the confusion that occurs when reading the books of Kings and Chronicles and trying to unravel the names used for the kings—especially when as many as three different names are used for the same king!

We will first of all look at the reigns of the three monarchs who succeeded King Ahab—his sons Ahaziah and Joram (who is also called Jehoram), and his daughter Athaliah, who was, as we shall see, one of the most evil women who has ever lived. Athaliah married Jehoram (who was also called Joram), who was the son of King Jehoshaphat of the Southern Kingdom of Judah. Athaliah's household must have been confusing—her husband had two names: Jehoram and Joram; and her brother had two names: Joram and Jehoram. And to confuse matters even further, she called her son Ahaziah after one of her brothers. Naming children after relatives is not uncommon and is still practised today.[1]

King Joram of the Northern Kingdom of Israel

Early in Chapter 5 we saw how, when King Ahab died in 853 BC, his son Ahaziah succeeded him as king. As we noted there, he reigned for only two years (one actual year), dying from injuries he sustained when he fell from the balcony of the roof of his palace in fulfilment of the word spoken by Elijah, because King Ahaziah had not sought counsel from God (2 Kings 1). Because he had no sons to succeed him, his brother Joram, who was also called Jehoram, became king of the Northern Kingdom of Israel in 852 BC.

Until the death of King Ahab, the king of Moab had paid annually a tribute of a hundred thousand lambs and the wool from a hundred thousand sheep to the king of the Northern Kingdom of Israel. Once Joram became king of the Northern Kingdom of Israel, he asked Jehoshaphat, the king of the Southern Kingdom of Judah, if he would help him go to war against Moab. They did so and were joined by the kingdom of Edom. This coalition then set out for Moab, but after marching for seven days they ran out of water and called for the prophet Elisha, who made it very clear to King Joram (who, remember, was the son of King Ahab and his wife Jezebel) that he would not have given him any word from God had it not been for his alliance with godly King Jehoshaphat of the Southern Kingdom of Judah.

Elisha instructed the coalition forces to dig ditches all over the dry stream bed, promising that even though they would not see any rain, this stream bed would be filled with water so that their army, cattle and pack animals would have plenty to drink. As a result, the triple alliance forces enjoyed an amazing victory over Moab, for when the Moabite army arose early the next day, they looked westwards and saw the morning sun reflected in the miraculously sent water. Since it reflected red, the Moabites thought it was blood and assumed that the three armies had destroyed each other. They decided to go and loot the camp, but when they reached it they were attacked by the triple alliance forces and were forced to retreat. Elisha had also told the coalition armies that they were to destroy the Moabite cities, cut down their fruit trees, stop their springs and scatter stones over every good piece of farmland. This is what they did as they chased the retreating Moabites. In desperation, the king of Moab offered his eldest son as a burnt offering to try to persuade his gods to turn the tide of the battle—but to no avail. Moab was thoroughly defeated.

As we saw in Chapter 5, King Joram of the Northern Kingdom of Israel was not as successful in defeating the Syrians, even with the help of his nephew, King Ahaziah of the Southern Kingdom of Judah, who was advised by his counsellors to join forces with him. When their armies clashed with the Syrian army in Ramoth Gilead, King Joram of the Northern Kingdom of Israel was wounded and returned to his palace in Jezreel to recover, and was soon joined by his nephew, King Ahaziah of the Southern Kingdom of Judah. King Joram's problem was then compounded when one of his officers, Jehu, led an insurrection against him. We saw how Jehu had been anointed king of the Northern Kingdom of Israel and that he began to fulfil God's command to kill all of King Ahab's descendants by murdering King Joram, who was King Ahab's son, and also King Ahaziah of the Southern Kingdom of Judah, who was King Ahab's grandson. King Ahaziah's body was buried in the royal tombs in the City of David in Jerusalem, but King Joram's corpse was cast into Naboth's field outside the city of Jezreel.

Queen Athaliah of the Southern Kingdom of Judah

Without doubt, Athaliah is one of the most evil characters that we meet in the Old Testament, yet few Christians and churchgoers know about her. In fact, the only thing we know of her background is that she was one of the daughters of Ahab—her mother's name is not recorded in the Bible in any of the genealogies.[2] Athaliah was married to King Jehoram of the Southern Kingdom of Judah who, as the eldest son, acceded to the throne when his father, King Jehoshaphat, died in 848 BC. Jehoram was thirty-two years old when he began to reign, and he reigned eight years (that is, seven actual years). He was not a good king, for as soon as he was in firm control of his kingdom he killed his brothers (all six of them!) and some of the princes of the Northern Kingdom of Israel (presumably their sons and whoever else was related to them). The Bible records that King Jehoram walked in the ways of the kings of the Northern Kingdom of Israel—he made places for pagan worship in the mountains and caused the inhabitants of Jerusalem to prostitute themselves. The Bible tells us in 2 Chronicles 21:6 that the reason why King Jehoram of the Southern Kingdom of Judah behaved in such a manner was because of his wife, Athaliah, whom it describes simply as 'the daughter of Ahab'.

Later in the same chapter (2 Chr. 21), we read that the prophet Elijah wrote a letter to King Jehoram of the Southern Kingdom of Judah, telling him that because he had behaved so badly, he would have a disease of the intestines. However, before the king began to suffer with this illness, the Philistines and Arabians invaded the Southern Kingdom of Judah and carried away not only the contents of the king's palace, but also his wives and all his sons, except his youngest—Ahaziah (who was also named Jehoahaz as well as Azariah). Elijah's prophecy was eventually fulfilled and the king died in severe pain, possibly of haemorrhoids. King Jehoram of the Southern Kingdom of Judah was not a popular monarch; the Bible records that he died 'to no one's sorrow' (2 Chr. 21:20, NKJV) and that, although he was buried in the City of David, he was not buried in the tombs of the kings.

When King Jehoram died, his son Ahaziah was made king of the Southern Kingdom of Judah. If we are not careful, reading the Bible about this king can lead to confusion because he is referred to not only as Ahaziah (2 Chr. 22:1), but also as Jehoahaz (2 Chr. 21:17) and as Azariah (2 Chr. 22:6). Furthermore, in 2 Chronicles 22:2 we are informed that he was forty-two years old when he became king. Most scholars regard this as a copyist's error[3] which is easily made due to the small stroke that differentiates two Hebrew letters.[4] In 2 Kings 8:26 King Ahaziah's age is correctly recorded as twenty-two.[5]

King Ahaziah of the Southern Kingdom of Judah reigned for only one year, and was a wicked king, just like his father, King Jehoram. The Bible gives us the reason for this: King Ahaziah was advised by his mother, Athaliah, and also by the counsellors who had advised his father, King Jehoram. As we saw in the previous section, on the advice of these counsellors King Ahaziah joined forces with King Joram of the Northern Kingdom of Israel in going to war with the king of Syria at Ramoth Gilead. King Joram was wounded and went to Jezreel to recover. When King Ahaziah of the Southern Kingdom of Judah went to visit him there, he was killed by Jehu. As soon as King Ahaziah was buried, Athaliah had all the royal heirs of the Southern Kingdom of Judah murdered. In other words, this evil woman was responsible for the deaths of her own grandchildren. However, one of her grandchildren was rescued: the baby Joash was taken by his aunt Jehosheba (who was also called Jehoshabeath), who was the daughter of King Jehoram of the Southern Kingdom of Judah and also the half-sister of King Ahaziah of the Southern Kingdom of Judah. Little Joash was hidden in the temple in Jerusalem for six years by Jehosheba and her husband Jehoiada, who was the high priest.

In the meantime, Joash's grandmother, Athaliah, ruled as queen. Although the Bible does not give the length of her reign, it can be calculated easily from other details that are given. We know that she became queen as soon as Jehu had killed King Ahaziah (in 841 BC) and that she reigned until Joash was crowned king of the Southern Kingdom of Judah when he was seven years old (in 835 BC). These dates fit exactly the statement in 2 Chronicles 22:12 that Joash had been hidden for six years before he was crowned king. All these figures indicate that Athaliah reigned for six years, from 841 to 835 BC. There is very little in the Bible about what happened during the reign of Queen Athaliah. The Bible refers to her as 'that wicked woman' in 2 Chronicles 24:7 (NKJV). In the same verse, we are told that her sons broke into the temple of God and used its sacred objects for the Baals. The thought of temple items being used in Baal worship is almost too abhorrent to imagine. But Queen Athaliah's reign would soon come to an end.

It was Jehoiada the priest who came up with the plan to overthrow Queen Athaliah. As we have seen, he and his wife Jehosheba hid their nephew Joash, who was the only male descendant of King Jehoram of the Southern Kingdom of Judah, in the temple at Jerusalem for six years while Joash's grandmother, Athaliah, ruled as queen. How close to disappearing was the throne of David from which the Lord Jesus Christ was to come and reign! Just one little six-year-old boy was left alive of David's line. It looked as though Satan himself had used this evil woman, Athaliah, to extinguish the royal line of David and, in turn, to stop the birth of the Lion of the tribe of Judah who would descend from this line and one day crush Satan's head.

After keeping Joash hidden for six years, Jehoiada asked the officers in charge of the royal bodyguard and those in charge of the palace guards to come to the temple. He made them promise under oath not to reveal what he planned to do. He then showed them Joash and told them that this was the son of the late King Ahaziah. Jehoiada then told the soldiers what he wanted them to do when the priests and Levites came on duty on the Sabbath. He told them to guard Joash so that he could be crowned king. The officers and soldiers obeyed Jehoiada and, on the Sabbath, Jehoiada crowned Joash king of the Southern Kingdom of Judah and gave him a copy of the laws governing kingship. Joash was then anointed king by Jehoiada and his sons, and everyone shouted, 'Long live the king!'

When Queen Athaliah heard the people cheering and shouting for King Joash, she rushed to the temple where the people had gathered. When she saw the people celebrating and rejoicing, and heard the trumpeters and musicians, she tore her clothes and shouted, 'Treason! Treason!' Jehoiada did not want Queen Athaliah killed in the temple area, so he ordered the army officers to take her to the palace and execute her there, which they did. Jehoiada also instructed the officers to kill anyone who tried to rescue her. It would have been very surprising if anyone had tried to rescue Athaliah, as she was such an evil woman. In fact, 2 Chronicles 23:21 informs us that all the people rejoiced that Athaliah had been killed.

King Joash of the Southern Kingdom of Judah

Now the scene is set for little Joash to enter the Southern Kingdom of Judah as king, where would reign for the next thirty-nine years—from 835 to 796 BC. The one thing we have to realize about King Joash, however, is that he was influenced and instructed by his uncle Jehoiada, the husband of Jehosheba, for 2 Chronicles 24:2 states quite clearly that Joash did what was pleasing to the Lord as long as Jehoiada was alive. Jehoiada's influence can be seen, for as soon as King Joash began to reign, Jehoiada made the people enter into a covenant with the Lord that they would be the Lord's people. This resulted in the people entering the temple of Baal and smashing the idols and altars, killing Mattan the priest of Baal and tearing down the temple of Baal. Jehoiada then reintroduced temple worship into the temple, even putting guards on duty at the temple gates to keep out anyone who was ritually unclean.

By the twenty-third year of the reign of King Joash of the Southern Kingdom of Judah, no repairs had been made to the temple, so King Joash called Jehoiada and the other priests and asked them why this was the case. This was in spite of the fact that the priests had received money from the people in connection with the sacrifices being made. King Joash would have been about thirty years old at the time; clearly he was still concerned about what might be called 'the things of the Lord'. At this meeting between the king and the priests it was agreed that the repairs to the temple should start and, to pay for this, a collection box would be used to collect the money that was brought by the people to the temple. This box was placed at the temple gate and as soon as there was a large amount of money in the box, it was opened and the silver in it was melted down to pay for the materials used to repair the temple and also to pay the workmen. The Bible records that the people involved with the work were so honest that no receipts were necessary to account for any of the purchases or payments. The Bible also informs us that 'about this time' the Syrians attacked Jerusalem and King Joash took all the sacred objects dedicated by his fathers (Jehoshaphat, Jehoram and Ahaziah) and the gifts he himself had dedicated and all the gold found in the treasures of the temple and the royal palace, and sent them to the king of Syria, who then withdrew from Jerusalem.

Our cemeteries are proof that no one lives for ever. The ultimate statistic is that one in one people die. And so it came to pass that at the ripe old age of one hundred and thirty, Jehoiada, King Joash's trusted old uncle, friend and confidant, died and went to be with his Maker. Jehoiada was a well-loved and respected man, and in recognition of the service he had done for the people, for God and for the temple, he was buried in the royal tombs in the City of David in Jerusalem. This was equivalent to giving him a state funeral. But once Jehoiada was dead, the leaders of the Southern Kingdom of Judah persuaded King Joash to listen to them, and so the people stopped worshipping in the temple and began to worship idols and images of the goddess Asherah. God's anger turned against Jerusalem and he sent prophets to warn the people to return to him, but they refused to listen to them. Then the Lord sent Zechariah the son of

Jehoiada to speak to the people. A careful look at Joash's family tree in Figure 3 on page 89 will show that Zechariah was also Jehosheba's son and so was also King Joash's half-cousin. This time, King Joash joined the crowds in refusing to listen to the message that the prophet of the Lord was speaking, and on the king's orders, the people stoned Zechariah to death. It would appear that the king had forgotten all the kindness that Zechariah's parents had shown him in hiding him from the evil clutches of his wicked grandmother Athaliah, and all the loyal service that Jehoiada had given him over the years when he was king. His half-cousin Zechariah's last words to the king were, 'May the LORD see what you are doing and punish you!' (GNT).

It was not long before the Lord did punish King Joash, for in the autumn following the murder of Zechariah, the Syrian army attacked Jerusalem, killed all the leaders and took large amounts of plunder back to Damascus. The Bible records that although King Joash's army was large, the Lord allowed it to be defeated by the smaller Syrian army because the people had abandoned the Lord. In this way, Zechariah's dying prayer was answered: God punished King Joash. Furthermore, King Joash was severely wounded, and two of his officials killed him in his bed to avenge the murder of Zechariah. After a thirty-nine-year reign, King Joash was buried in the City of David in Jerusalem, but not in the royal tombs. King Joash's son, Amaziah, became king of the Southern Kingdom of Judah in his place in 796 BC. As soon as King Amaziah was firmly established as king of the Southern Kingdom of Judah, he executed the officials who had killed his father, King Joash.

Summary and conclusion

From the time when King Ahab of the Northern Kingdom of Israel died in 853 BC to when his great-grandson Joash was crowned king of the Southern Kingdom of Judah in 835 BC was a mere eighteen years. During this time, two of King Ahab's sons reigned over the Northern Kingdom of

Israel—Ahaziah and then Joram. We saw that both these sons followed in the footsteps of their parents and worshipped Baal.

We then considered one of the most evil characters that we meet in the Old Testament: Athaliah—the daughter of King Ahab of the Northern Kingdom of Israel who was married to King Jehoram of the Southern Kingdom of Judah, and who would stop at nothing to be the sole ruler of the Southern Kingdom of Judah. When King Jehoram died, he was succeeded by his son Ahaziah, who was killed by Jehu. As soon as King Ahaziah was buried, his mother, Athaliah, had all the heirs to the Southern Kingdom of Judah murdered. Only one grandchild escaped: Joash, who was hidden for six years in the temple by his aunt Jehosheba and her husband, the priest Jehoiada.

After six years, Joash was crowned king of the Southern Kingdom of Judah, and at his coronation, Queen Athaliah was taken captive and executed. Under Jehoiada's influence the altars of Baal and the idols in the temple were destroyed and temple worship was reintroduced. However, when Jehoiada died, King Joash turned away from following the Lord, even when the Lord sent prophets to rebuke him. Finally, the Lord sent King Joash's half-cousin, Zechariah, to warn him, but he took no notice of him and instructed the people to stone him to death. Zechariah's last words were a plea that the Lord might see what King Joash was doing and punish him. The Lord answered Zechariah's prayer, for a few months later a small Syrian army invaded Jerusalem, and King Joash was severely wounded. Two of his officials then murdered him because of the way he had treated Zechariah.

What lesson can we learn from the life of King Joash? The answer to that question is really the answer we give to this question: Why do we follow and serve God? Is it because we have a relative who leads and guides us as King Joash had? Do we follow the Lord because we are like Jehoiada and *want* to follow God and serve him? Remember how the people gave Jehoiada the equivalent of a state funeral because of his service to the Lord. I am sure he did not serve the Lord because he was hoping for that; he served the Lord because he loved the Lord and wanted to serve the Lord. How about you?

I have seen many young people in churches who appear to follow God when their relatives (particularly their grandparents) are alive and give them godly advice; however, when those relatives die, the young people stop going to church and want nothing more to do with the Lord and his ways. They behave just as King Joash did when his old uncle Jehoiada died. So how about you? Do you serve the Lord because you have a relative who influences you? Would you still serve the Lord if that relative died? Or have you a heart like King Joash?

NOTES

1 In my own family there are a number of people who have been given the name Joseph, and with one exception they are called Joe. My father, Joe White, was named after his uncle, Joe Pearce. One of my father's sisters married a Joe Meanley and they named their son Joe. To avoid any confusion and to distinguish who is being referred to in the family, all those with the name Joe are called by their Christian name *and* their surname. Hence there is Joe Pearce, Joe White, Joe Meanley and Joe Meanley Junior. My sister's grandson is called Joseph, and he was named after my father, his great-grandfather. My second name is Joseph, after my father.

2 It is interesting to note that in the eighth edition of Robert Young's *Analytical Concordance to the Holy Bible* (London: United Society for Christian Literature/Lutterworth Press, 1973), Athaliah is recorded as being the daughter of Jezebel, wife of Ahab, even though there is no Bible verse to prove this relationship. In the family tree in Figure 3 on page 89, I have shown Athaliah as being descended from the union of King Ahab with his wife Jezebel, although the reader should bear in mind that this may not actually be the case.

3 See 'Ahaziah of Judah', Wikipedia, https://en.wikipedia.org/wiki/Ahaziah_of_Judah.

4 Footnote on 2 Chr. 22:2 in *The MacArthur Study Bible ESV* (Wheaton, IL: Crossway, 2010).

5 Ahaziah could not have been forty-two when he ascended the throne, as his father Jehoram was only forty-four years old when he died. It should be noted that in 2 Chr. 21:20 it states that Jehoram was thirty-two years old when he became king and that he reigned for eight years (that is, seven actual years). To understand this verse completely, we need to be aware that Jehoram was thirty-two years old when he began to reign, but he was

co-regent with his father, Jehoshaphat, for five years—that is, from 853 to 848 BC. He then reigned on his own for seven years, making him forty-four years old when he died.

The Lion on the throne of David

I n this book we have looked at some of the kings in the Old Testament who were rogues but who wore royal robes. No matter what excuses they made for themselves or we may make for them, the stories of the lives of these kings of the Northern Kingdom of Israel and of the Southern Kingdom of Judah are very sad tales indeed. These kings (and queens) who ruled the Northern Kingdom of Israel and the Southern Kingdom of Judah included idolaters, liars, thieves, adulterers and murderers; almost every one of them broke God's commandments, seemingly without any fear that God would punish them either in this life or the next. They cared nothing for God's rules and simply wanted to rule for their own ends. Without doubt, they thought that they were above the Law—until the Lord showed them otherwise.

It is true that one or two of these rogues about whom I have written had redeeming features. King Omri, for example, was a great military commander, and he also built Samaria, the capital city of the Northern Kingdom of Israel. His son, Ahab, was also renowned for his architectural abilities. King Joash, under the guidance of his uncle Jehoiada, not only reintroduced temple worship, but also supervised the repair of the temple in Jerusalem. However, so many of them were not followers of the Lord. King Omri married off his son, Ahab, to the evil Jezebel, who was a Phoenician princess, the daughter of Ethbaal, the king of Tyre. Their children (Kings Ahaziah and Joram) did not follow the Lord. The influence of King Ahab and his wife Jezebel on King Jehoshaphat's son, King Jehoram of the Southern Kingdom of Judah, who was married to their daughter Athaliah, was profound. King Jehoram killed his six brothers to make sure of his position as king and he was so disliked by his subjects that when he died, it was to 'no one's sorrow'.

This final chapter is 'the odd one out' because it is *not* about a rogue. It is about the Lord Jesus Christ, the perfect man, the only man who has never sinned. Although Jesus Christ is the King of kings, when he lived on this earth he did not wear royal robes and he did not live in a royal palace. In fact, we shall see in this chapter how the Lord Jesus Christ is a complete contrast to the kings that we have looked at in the rest of the book. Those kings were rogues and are now dead; the Lord Jesus Christ was not a rogue and, although he was crucified by the Roman authorities, he rose from the dead, is still alive and he lives for evermore!

Jesus Christ was not a rogue

The first thing we notice about the Lord Jesus Christ is that, unlike all the other kings that we have looked at in detail in this book—Omri, Ahab, Jehu and Joash—he was *not* a rogue. We can appreciate this as we read the Gospel stories that give us an account of the life of the Lord Jesus Christ. There is not one story in these accounts that tells of his being a rogue—far from it! In every single dealing with his family, friends, followers, the Jewish authorities and members of the Roman occupation, the Lord Jesus Christ shines through the pages of the Scriptures as the opposite of a rogue—as a kind, honest, truthful, helpful, loving person who put the cares and needs of others before his own. If you doubt this, read the Gospel accounts of Matthew, Mark, Luke and John and see for yourself that he was not a rogue.

Jesus Christ was not born in and did not live in a palace

The Gospel of Matthew gives the genealogy of the Lord Jesus Christ through King David back to Abraham. Andrew Peterson has put the genealogy of Jesus Christ in Matthew chapter 1 to music and it is well worth listening to.[1] When the angel Gabriel told Mary that she was pregnant, he told her to call her child Jesus, that the Lord God would give Jesus the throne of his father King David, that Jesus would reign for ever and that of his kingdom there would be no end. Unlike King Omri, the Lord Jesus Christ had a genealogy—Matthew was able to trace Jesus' family tree back over two thousand years to Abraham; and in his Gospel, Luke was able to trace Jesus' family history all the way back to Adam, the first person made by God.

The Lord Jesus Christ was not born in a palace, nor did he live in a palace as King Solomon or King Omri did. When the so-called Wise Men came seeking the Lord Jesus Christ, they first went to Jerusalem, the capital city, asking where the king of the Jews was. The religious leaders searched the Scriptures and realized that the prophets had predicted that he would not be born in the capital city of Jerusalem, but in Bethlehem, which at the time of Jesus' birth was a village about 5½ miles (9 km) south of Jerusalem. When Jesus was born, his mother laid him in a manger—a feeding trough for the animals—because there was no room for him and his family anywhere else in the house where they were staying. He was not laid in an ivory bed the like of which King Ahab and Queen Jezebel lay in. Furthermore, during his ministry, he told his followers that although foxes have holes and birds have nests in which to live, he had no place in which to lay his head. In other words, he had no house that he could call home; he certainly had no palace, even though he was and is the King of kings.

Jesus Christ did not wear royal robes

Not only did the Lord Jesus Christ not live in a royal palace, but he did not wear royal robes. We realize this when we read the accounts of the crucifixion: he had a few garments, including a seamless tunic for which the soldiers cast lots (that is, gambled) to decide who should have it. Those who were executed by means of crucifixion were crucified totally naked—that is why the soldiers divided Jesus' clothes among themselves.

Contrary to what is frequently depicted in paintings and effigies of the crucified Christ, possibly the only thing that he wore was the crown of thorns; there is no record of the crown of thorns having been removed when Jesus was crucified; but, on the other hand, there is no record of its being left on his head.

Christians are often ridiculed for believing things that are 'pie in the sky'—things that we cannot see and which seemingly cannot possibly be true. This is because those who are not Christians fail to understand that many things taught in the Bible are unseen because they are symbolic. Although the Lord Jesus Christ did not wear royal robes, covering him was an unseen robe of righteousness, and this unseen royal robe covers us when we are Christians. The moment we repent of our sins and trust the Lord Jesus Christ as our Saviour, our unseen symbolic filthy rags of unrighteousness are replaced by Christ's unseen symbolic robe of righteousness. Christians understand this, but unfortunately non-Christians cannot (and, sometimes, will not) come to terms with this. So, in a sense, it can be said of Christians that they are truly rogues in royal robes—sinners whose unseen symbolic filthy rags of unrighteousness have been replaced by Christ's unseen symbolic royal robes of righteousness.

Jesus Christ, the head of an unseen army of followers

Just as the kings that we have studied in this book were at the head of armies, so the Lord Jesus Christ is the head of an army. This army is composed of those who have trusted in him for their salvation. In contrast to the armies in the Old Testament, the people who are in the army of the Lord Jesus Christ are not conscripts but volunteers; they serve the Lord voluntarily and their reward in this life is the fruit of the Spirit—love, joy, peace, longsuffering, gentleness, goodness, faith, meekness and temperance; and their reward at the end of their life on earth is eternal life with their Lord. In the book of Revelation, the Apostle John had a vision of the army of the Lord which was so great that no one could number it and was composed of people from every nation—it is not national, but international. Furthermore, membership of the Lord's army is not restricted to gender, as it was in the Old Testament, but is open to men *and* women.

I have already pointed out that some of the things that are taught in the Scriptures are symbolic and not to be taken literally. The armour that we, as soldiers of Christ our King, are to wear is symbolic and is described in detail for us by the Apostle Paul in his letter to the Ephesians:

Therefore take up the whole armour of God, that you may be able to withstand in the evil day, and having done all, to stand firm. Stand therefore, having fastened on the belt of truth, and having put on the breastplate of righteousness, and, as shoes for your feet, having put on the readiness given by the gospel of peace. In all circumstances take up the shield of faith, with which you can extinguish all the flaming darts of the evil one; and take the helmet of salvation, and the sword of the Spirit, which is the word of God, praying at all times in the Spirit, with all prayer and supplication. (Eph. 6:13–18a, ESV)

Some of the invisible symbolic clothing, such as our robe of righteousness, is given to us at salvation, but some of the other invisible symbolic clothing, such as our armour, has to be put on. As with so much of the Bible, the Scriptures that it contains have to be interpreted carefully.

Jesus Christ, sitting on the throne of David

In 2 Samuel 7:16 the Lord promised King David through the prophet Nathan that David's kingdom and throne would be established for ever. When the angel Gabriel told Mary that she was pregnant with Jesus, he told her, among other things, that 'the Lord God will give to him [Jesus] the throne of his father David, and he will reign over the house of Jacob for ever, and of his kingdom there will be no end' (Luke 1:32–33, ESV).

We saw in Chapter 6 how close to disappearing was the throne of

David from which the Lord Jesus Christ was to come and reign. Just one little six-year-old boy, Joash, was left alive of David's line. It looked as though Satan had used Joash's evil grandmother, Athaliah, to extinguish the royal line of David. But God had promised David that he would never lack anyone to sit on the throne of David, and God kept his promise. God had raised up David, and as we read the Bible we can see how he kept David's line unbroken even in the days of Athaliah.

This is the reason why Matthew's Gospel gives the genealogy of Jesus back to King David, for it shows the unbroken line of the throne of David from the Lord Jesus Christ back to King David. That is why the angel Gabriel could say that the Lord God would give to Jesus the throne 'of his father David'—for it was his by (birth)right. And with this throne went the kingdom—the kingdom of Israel, which is God's kingdom. This is an area where Jesus' disciples failed to understand the purpose of his coming—they thought that he would establish an earthly kingdom. This explains their bewilderment at Jesus' teachings about his establishing a heavenly kingdom. Even after his resurrection and just before his ascension, the disciples were still asking the Lord Jesus Christ when he was going to restore the kingdom to Israel; they were still expecting Jesus to establish and to sit on the throne of David in Jerusalem at that time. But Jesus' kingdom is not an earthly kingdom, as we have seen in the previous sections of this chapter. His kingdom is a heavenly kingdom, and it is composed of all those who have put their trust in him for their salvation.

Jesus Christ, the Lion and the Lamb

The Apostle John has a beautiful vision of the Lord Jesus Christ recorded for us in Revelation chapter 5. It is a very strange vision, for he sees the Lord Jesus Christ not only as the Lion of the tribe of Judah, but also as a Lamb that has been slain. What a wonderful picture of the Lord Jesus Christ: a conquering lion and a sacrificial lamb, at the same time. And this is what the Lord Jesus Christ is. He is the King of kings; and, according to Psalm 8, one day all things will be under his feet. He is also the sacrificial lamb, for on the cross he was slain for our sins.

Summary and conclusion

The Lord Jesus Christ is both King and Saviour. No wonder the Apostle John heard every creature in heaven and on earth saying: 'To him who sits on the throne and to the Lamb be blessing and honour and glory and might for ever and ever!' (Rev. 5:13, ESV).

If we are rogues dressed in his royal robes of righteousness, then let us, too, give blessing and honour and glory and might to the Lord Jesus Christ, our King and our Lamb, for ever and ever!

NOTES

1 Andrew Peterson, 'Matthew's Begats', YouTube, 13 December 2008, https://www.youtube.com/watch?v=snURV57_tjo

Events that took place in the year 841 BC

- Fulfilling Elijah's prophecy, King Jehoram of the Southern Kingdom of Judah died, in severe pain, of an intestinal disease, possibly haemorrhoids. He was not a popular monarch; the Bible records that he died 'to no one's sorrow' (2 Chr. 21:20, NKJV) and that, although he was buried in the City of David, he was not buried in the tombs of the kings.
- Jehu killed King Joram, king of the Northern Kingdom of Israel, and reigned as king of the Northern Kingdom of Israel in his place (2 Kings 9:23–26).
- Ahaziah, King Jehoram's youngest son, became king of the Southern Kingdom of Judah and reigned for part of the year. He was killed by King Jehu and was buried in the royal tombs in the City of David in Jerusalem (2 Kings 9:27–29).
- Jezebel, King Ahab's widow, was murdered by being thrown out of a window of her palace in Jezreel on the orders of King Jehu (2 Kings 9:30–37).
- By murdering all the heirs to the Southern Kingdom of Judah on the death of her son King Ahaziah, Athaliah became queen of the Southern Kingdom of Judah.
- King Jehu of the Northern Kingdom of Israel paid tribute to King Shalmaneser III of Assyria. Although not recorded in the Bible, this event is depicted on the Black Obelisk of Shalmaneser III which is located in the British Museum in London.

Kings of the Northern Kingdom of Israel[1]

KING	OVERLAPPING REIGNS (BC)	DATES OF REIGN (BC)
Jeroboam I		931/30–910/9
Nadab		910/9–909/8
Baasha		909/8–886/85
Elah		886/85–885/84
Zimri		885/84
Tibni		885/84–880
Omri	885/84–880	880–874/73
Ahab		874/73–853
Ahaziah		853—852
Joram		852–841
Jehu		841–814/13
Jehoahaz		814/13–798
Jehoash		798–782/81
Jeroboam II	793/92–782/81	782/81–753
Zechariah		753–752
Shallum		752
Menahem		752–742/41
Pekahiah		742/41–740/39
Pekah	752–740/39	740/39–732/31
Hoshea		732/31–723/22

1 This table is taken from Appendix B, in Edwin R. Thiele, *The Mysterious Numbers of the Hebrew Kings*, new rev. edn (Grand Rapids, MI: Kregel, 1994), p. 217.

Kings of the Southern Kingdom of Judah[1]

KING	DATES OF CO-REGENCY (BC)	DATES OF REIGN (BC)
Rehoboam		931/930–913
Abijah		913–911/10
Asa		911/10–870/69
Jehoshaphat	872/71–870/69	870/69–848
Jehoram	853–848	848–841
Ahaziah		841
Athaliah		841–835
Joash		835–796
Amaziah		796–767
Azariah (Uzziah)	792/91–767	767–740/39
Jotham	750–740/39	740/39–732/31
Ahaz	735–732/31	732/31–716/15
Hezekiah		716/15–687/86
Manasseh	697/96–687/86	687/86–643/42
Amon		643/42–641/40
Josiah		641/40–609
Jeoahaz		609
Jehoiakim		609–598
Jehoiachin		598–597
Zedekiah		597–586

1 This table is taken from Appendix B, in Edwin R. Thiele, *The Mysterious Numbers of the Hebrew Kings*, new rev. edn (Grand Rapids, MI: Kregel, 1994), p. 217.